imental
Formats.2

Books
Brochures
Catalogs

Roger Fawcett-Tang

Experimental Formats.2 A

Contents

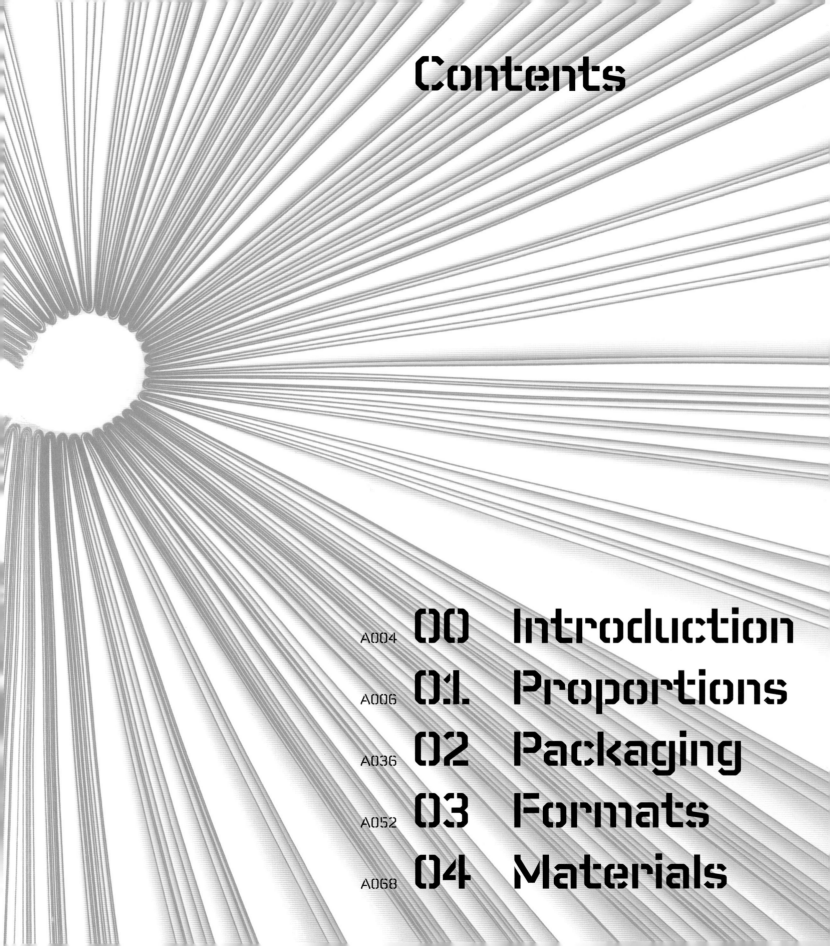

Introduction

Not long ago, the bookshop was an almost hallowed repository of knowledge, with a hushed stillness and the musty aroma of aging volumes sitting patiently on oak bookcases. Such shops do still exist, but sadly their days are numbered. Shopping malls are now populated by book megastores and hip book boutiques in which you are confronted with a sprawling mass of books, catalogs, and magazines all fighting for your attention. The choice is vast and the variety seemingly endless. The hush has been replaced with the blare of this week's Number One and the surround-sound special FX of the latest DVD release. The smells of aging leather and wood have been replaced with the aroma of a freshly brewed double skinny latte with vanilla on top.

However, this globalized megadom does have a positive side; it has ensured that the production of books and other printed matter has thrived. The quantity and quality of titles available is now at an all-time high, with every imaginable specialism being catered for with a daunting breadth of choice. This has led to a battle for the consumer's attention, especially within the visual "coffee table book" market. Adding value to a volume has become the weapon of choice, whether this be through a CD-ROM stuck in or onto the book, or an elaborate packaging device that makes the title literally stand out from its competitors.

Not only is the world of publicly available books becoming more lavish, catalogs and brochures are following suit. The designer, again, is always striving to make his or her client's printed matter stand out from the competition. As more and more businesses are seeing the benefits of an online presence as a cost-effective way of promoting their company, printed matter needs to work much harder than ever before. This does not just mean visual pyrotechnics; equally, it can mean good old-fashioned quality. A beautiful and lavish publication has prestige and can help to establish a very strong market value for the company.

Over the pages of this double-hinged edition, selected work ranges from big-budget, eight-color, lavish productions to small-run, two-color leaflets. This breadth of work is very important. It is not always necessary to have a megabudget to achieve a successful solution; sometimes financial restrictions can help to focus the designer's mind on alternative methods of binding, printing, or formats. A short print run can make complex handfinishing a viable option, whereas bigger 10,000 or 100,000 print runs can restrict this freedom and often extinguish a great many creative possibilities before the first print quote is sent out. Conversely, big print runs can be beneficial for some production techniques and finishes. Moving beyond standard lithographic printing methods, certain packaging systems only become a possibility if the print run is high enough to cover any bespoke machining and tool set-up costs.

This book is not just about the myriad production techniques at the designer's disposal—it is also important to consider the physical dimensions of a job, whether larger or smaller, wider or narrower. The default for most brochures and catalogs is the standard of A4 ($210 \times 297\,$mm/$8^{1}/_{8} \times 11.^{11}/_{16}$in), usually saddle stitched, and with an average of 24 pages. Anything that can break the norm will generate interest and stand out from the masses. Sometimes the simplest thing can transform a job: text pages cut to a smaller size than the cover, an unexpected fold, or a disorientating navigation system. The main thing is to always push, to experiment and think differently, while not losing sight of the client's wishes and the demands of the original brief. On the odd occasion a designer is given total freedom to develop a project, it is still important not to alienate the reader, but to make them feel they are involved— the rewards for all concerned will be far greater.

A01.1/
porti

open
discover
explore

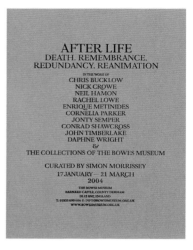

Design	2GD/2Graphic:Design	Design	3 Deep Design	Design	3 Deep Design	Design	A2-GRAPHICS/SW/HK
Project	ToC.2GDIV	Project	Amplification. Jeff Busby	Project	Tourism Victoria	Project	After Life
Size	200 × 100mm	Size	31.8 × 21.5mm	Size	31.8 × 21.5mm		Death. Remembrance.
	(7⅞ × 4in)		(1.2½ × 8½in)		(1.2½ × 8½in)		Redundancy. Reanimation
Pages	128	Pages	48	Pages	64	Size	252 × 190mm
Year	2000	Year	2002	Year	2004		(9³/₃₂ × 7³¹/₆₄in)
Origin	Denmark	Origin	Australia	Origin	Australia	Pages	72
						Year	2004
						Origin	UK

Go to: A071

Go to: B020

Go to: B021

Go to: B049

Christine Borland
Cai Guo-Qiang
Charles Crumb
Marlene Dumas
Susan Hiller
William Kentridge
Paul McCarthy
Elizabeth Manchester
Daniela Steinfeld
Jon Thompson

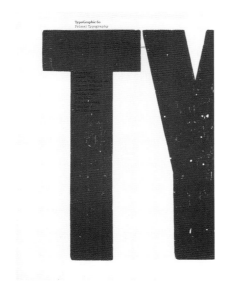

TypoGraphic 60
Primal Typography

Anna Barriball
David Musgrave

Recog

Edwina Ashton
David Mackintosh

Design	**A2-GRAPHICS/SW/HK**	Design	**A2-GRAPHICS/SW/HK**	Design	**A2-GRAPHICS/SW/HK**	Design	**Atelier Roger Pfund**
Project	Apparition: the Action of Appearing	Project	ISTD TypoGraphic 60 "Primal Typography"	Project	Recognition	Project	Hundert T Variationen
Size	21.7 ×1.56mm (8^{35}/$_{64}$ × 6^9/$_{64}$in)	Size	297 × 21.0mm (1.1.^{11}/$_{16}$ × 8^{53}/$_{64}$in)	Size	21.0 × 1.58mm (8^{53}/$_{64}$ × 6^{15}/$_{64}$mm)	Size	230 × 1.70mm (9^1/$_{16}$ × 6^3/$_4$in)
Pages	80	Pages	64	Pages	128	Pages	240
Year	2003	Year	2003	Year	2003	Year	2000
Origin	UK	Origin	UK	Origin	UK	Origin	Germany

Go to: A072

Go to: B058–B059

Go to: B030

Go to: A046

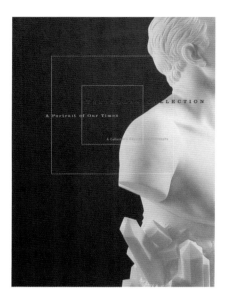
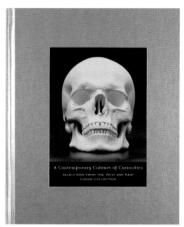

Amat Finques → Créixer, continuar, actualitzar, conèixer, confiar, escoltar, entendre, informar, assessorar, cuidar, ajudar, oferir, trobar, mantenir, gestionar, analitzar, rendibilitzar, exigir, optimitzar, consolidar → Crecer, continuar, actualizar, conocer, confiar, escuchar, entender, informar, asesorar, cuidar, ayudar, ofrecer, encontrar, mantener, gestionar, analizar, rentabilizar, exigir, optimizar, consolidar → Growth, continuation, actualisation, knowledge, advice, trust, listening, understanding, information, care, help, offers, finding, upkeep, management, analysis, profits, demands, optimisation, consolidation.

Design	**Aufuldish & Warinner**	Design	**Aufuldish & Warinner**	Design	**Aufuldish & Warinner**	Design	**Base Design**
Project	The Logan Collection: A Portrait of our Times A Collector's Odyssey and Philosophy	Project	A Contemporary Cabinet of Curiosities: Selections from the Vicki and Kent Logan Collection	Project	How Extraordinary that the World Exists!/Sudden Glory	Project	Amat Finques
						Size	300 × 230mm
Size	292 × 21.4mm	Size	235 × 1.84mm	Size	1.85 ×1.33mm		(1.1^{13}/$_{16}$ × 9^{3}/$_{64}$in)
	(1.1.1/2 × 8^{27}/$_{64}$in)		(9^{1}/$_{4}$ × 7^{1}/$_{4}$in)		(7^{9}/$_{32}$ × 5^{15}/$_{64}$in)	Pages	1.6
				Pages	1.20	Year	2000
Pages	224	Pages	52	Year	2002	Origin	Spain/Belgium/USA
Year	2002	Year	2001	Origin	USA		
Origin	USA	Origin	USA				

| Go to: | B053 | Go to: | B072 | Go to: | B073 | Go to: | B051 |

Design	**Base Design**	Design	**Base Design**	Design	**Base Design**	Design	**Nick Bell/Sacha Davison/**
Project	Serge Leblon	Project	Women'secret	Project	Women'secret		**Tom Elsner/Hilla Neske**
Size	255 × 212mm		Look Book:		Look Book:	Project	STD TypoGraphic 52
	(10¹/₃₂ × 8¹¹/₃₂in)		Spring/Summer 2003		Automne 03		"Other Values, Plus Ça"
Pages	68	Size	205 × 143mm	Size	210 × 152mm	Size	240 × 170mm
Year	2000		(8⁵/₆₄ × 5⁵/₈in)		(8⁵³/₆₄ × 5³¹/₃₂in)		(9⁷/₁₆ × 6³/₄in)
Origin	Belgium/Spain/USA	Pages	24 + 16	Pages	6 × folded posters	Pages	40
		Year	2003	Year	2003	Year	1998
		Origin	Spain/Belgium/USA	Origin	Spain/Belgium/USA	Origin	UK

Go to: B036   Go to: B044   Go to: A064   Go to: B060

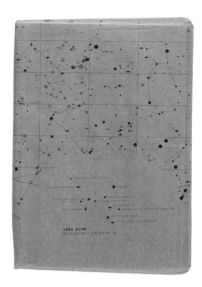

Design	**Benzin**	Design	**Blast**	Design	**Bohatsch Graphic Design**	Design	**Irma Boom**
Project	Super: Welcome to Graphic Wonderland	Project	Workout 2004	Project	Delugan_Meissl 2	Project	Gutenberg-Galaxie II
Size	240 × 166mm ($9^7/_{16}$ × $6^{17}/_{32}$in)	Size	105 × 148mm ($4^9/_{64}$ × $5^{53}/_{64}$in)	Size	227 × 164mm ($8^{15}/_{16}$ × $6^{29}/_{64}$in)	Size	290 × 193mm ($11.1^{13}/_{32}$ × $7^{19}/_{32}$in)
Pages	412	Pages	16 + 72	Pages	156 + 184	Pages	2 × 208
Year	2003	Year	2003	Year	2001	Year	2002
Origin	Switzerland	Origin	UK	Origin	Austria	Origin	The Netherlands

Go to: A049

Go to: B045

Go to: B040–B041

Go to: A041 B042–B043 B070

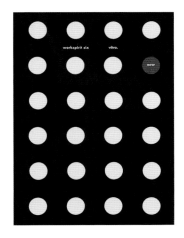

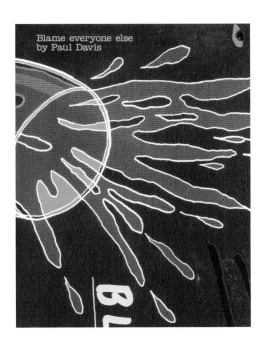

Design	**Irma Boom**
Project	Light Years:
	Zumtobel 2000 1950
Size	223 × 192mm
	(8²⁵/₃₂ × 7³⁵/₆₄in)
Pages	624
Year	2000
Origin	The Netherlands

Go to: B011

Design	**Irma Boom**
Project	Workspirit Six
Size	235 × 170mm
	(9¹/₄ × 6³/₄in)
Pages	176
Year	1998
Origin	The Netherlands

Go to: B069

Design	**Browns**
Project	Blame Everyone Else
	by Paul Davis
Size	332 × 248mm
	(7⅞ × 4in)
Pages	148
Year	2003
Origin	UK

Go to: A079

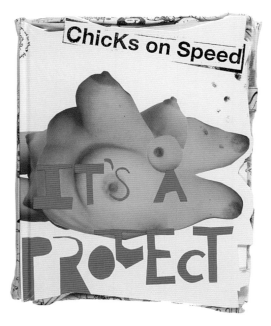

Design	**Build**	Design	**Cartlidge Levene**	Design	**Chicks on Speed**	Design	**COMA**
Project	"TRVL" Visual Travelogue	Project	9 Kean Street,	Project	It's a Project	Project	Glee: Painting Now
Size	257 × 185mm		Covent Garden	Size	325 × 265mm	Size	1.66 × 1.24mm
	(10¹/₈ × 7⁹/₃₂in)	Size	248 × 170mm		(12⁵¹/₆₄ × 10⁷/₁₆in)		(6¹⁷/₃₂ × 4³/₄in)
Pages	24		(9⁴⁹/₆₄ × 6³/₄in)	Pages	228	Pages	66 + 40
Year	2002	Pages	44 + 32	Year	2004	Year	2000
Origin	UK	Year	2001	Origin	USA	Origin	USA
		Origin	UK				

Go to: B008–B009   Go to: B047   Go to: A042 A057   B057   Go to: B052

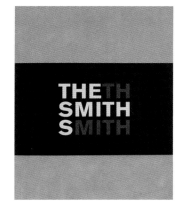

Design	**COMA**	Design	**The Designers Republic**	Design	**The Designers Republic**
Project	The Smiths	Project	ISTD TypoGraphic 58 "Too Much Noise Not Enough Time"	Project	3D→2D: Adventures in and out of Architecture
Size	21.5 × 170mm	Size	31.0 × 223mm	Size	230 × 340mm
	(8¹⁵/32 × 6³/4in)		(12¹³/64 × 8²⁵/32in)		(9³/64 × 13²⁵/64in)
Pages	112	Pages	32	Pages	198
Year	2002	Year	2002	Year	2000
Origin	USA	Origin	UK	Origin	UK

Go to: A078

Go to: A041

Go to: A065

Design	**Dowling Design**	Design	**Eg.G**	Design	**Eg.G**	Design	**Eggers + Diaper**
Project	Simon Patterson	Project	Onitsuka Tiger	Project	Quarantine	Project	Susan Hiller: Recall
	Colour Match screensaver	Size	150 × 160mm	Size	198 × 150mm	Size	266 × 225mm
Size	Ø 190mm		$(5^{29}/_{32} \times 6^{19}/_{64}$in)		$(7^{25}/_{32} \times 5^{29}/_{32}$in)		$(10^{15}/_{32} \times 8^{55}/_{64}$in)
	$(7^{31}/_{64}$in)	Pages	2 × 14	Pages	20	Pages	172
Pages	24	Year	2004	Year	2003	Year	2004
Year	2001	Origin	UK	Origin	UK	Origin	Germany
Origin	UK						

Go to: A044   Go to: B051   Go to: B049   Go to: B008

Design	Eggers + Diaper	Design	Eggers + Diaper	Design	Experimental Jetset	Design	Fabrica
Project	Spoon	Project	Witness	Project	The Peoples Art	Project	Mail Me
Size	210 × 300mm	Size	270 × 185mm	Size	185 × 127mm	Size	250 × 157 × 95mm
	(8⁵³/₆₄ × 11.¹³/₁₆in)		(10⁵/₈ × 7⁹/₃₂in)		(7⁹/₃₂ × 5in)		(9²⁷/₃₂ × 6³/₁₆ × 3³/₄in)
Pages	448	Pages	78	Pages	128	Pages	160 + 320
Year	2002	Year	2000	Year	2001	Year	2003
Origin	Germany	Origin	Germany	Origin	The Netherlands	Origin	Italy

Go to: A070

Go to: A047

Go to: A048

Go to: A039

Design	**Fabrica**
Project	2398 gr.: A Book About Food
Size	280 × 222mm
	(11 × 8³/₄in)
Pages	320
Year	2003
Origin	Italy

Design	**Faydherbe/De Vringer**
Project	Dolly-Book
Size	246 × 176mm
	(9¹¹/₁₆ × 6¹⁵/₁₆in)
Pages	32
Year	2001
Origin	The Netherlands

Design	**FL@33**
Project	Trans-form
Size	497 × 320mm
	(19.³⁷/₆₄ × 12¹⁹/₃₂in)
Pages	32
Year	2001
Origin	UK

Go to: A040   B028

Go to: A078

Go to: A058

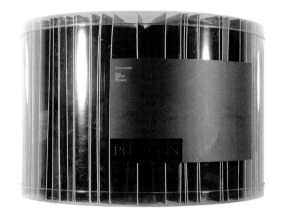

Design	**FL@33**		Design	**David James Associates**		Design
Project	Coup de Grace/		Project	The Order of Things		Project
	Zwischenstation		Size	185 × 260mm		Size
Size	225 × 155mm			(7⁹/₃₂ × 10¹⁵/₆₄in)		
	(8⁵⁵/₆₄ × 6⁷/₆₄in)		Pages	176		Pages
Pages	60 loose sheets		Year	2001		Year
Year	1997		Origin	UK		Origin
Origin	Germany					

Design **FL@33**
Project Coup de Grace/ Zwischenstation
Size 225 × 155mm (8⁵⁵/₆₄ × 6⁷/₆₄in)
Pages 60 loose sheets
Year 1997
Origin Germany

Design **David James Associates**
Project The Order of Things
Size 185 × 260mm (7⁹/₃₂ × 10¹⁵/₆₄in)
Pages 176
Year 2001
Origin UK

Design **Julia Hasting**
Project Gordon Matta-Clark
Size 257 × 256mm (10¹/₈ × 10⁵/₆₄in)
Pages 238
Year 2003
Origin UK

Go to: B037

Go to: A044   B061

Go to: B050

Design	**Intro**		Design	**The Kitchen**		
Project	The Colour of White		Project	"No"		
Size	263 × 263mm		Size	21.8 × 244mm		
	(10²³/₆₄ × 10²³/₆₄in)			(8¹⁹/₃₂ × 9³⁹/₆₄in)		
Pages	78		Pages	72		
Year	2001		Year	2002		
Origin	UK		Origin	UK		

Design   **Intro**
Project   The Colour of White
Size   263 × 263mm
                    ($10^{23}/_{64}$ × $10^{23}/_{64}$in)
Pages   78
Year   2001
Origin   UK

Design   **The Kitchen**
Project   "No"
Size   21.8 × 244mm
                    ($8^{19}/_{32}$ × $9^{39}/_{64}$in)
Pages   72
Year   2002
Origin   UK

Design   **The Kitchen**
Project   Levi's Red: Glass
Size   280 × 138mm
                    (1.1 × $5^{7}/_{16}$in)
Pages   20
Year   2001
Origin   UK

Go to: B007   Go to: B028   Go to: A054

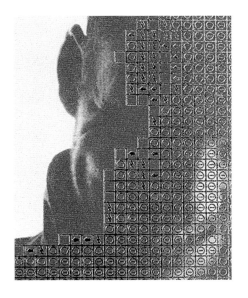

Design	**Made Thought**	Design	**Made Thought**	Design	**Made Thought**	Design	**Mode**
Project	Wasted Space?	Project	Bill Brandt catalog	Project	Thinking Big: Concepts for Twenty-First Century British Sculpture	Project	Lostrobots
Size	265 × 190mm	Size	224 × 165mm			Size	290 × 230mm
	(10.$7/16$ × 7$31/64$in)		(8$13/16$ × 6$31/64$in)	Size	215 × 154mm		(11.$13/32$ × 9$3/64$in)
Pages	24	Pages	32		(8$15/32$ × 6$4/64$in)	Pages	Variable
Year	2002	Year	2003	Pages	48 + 176	Year	2003
Origin	UK	Origin	UK	Year	2002	Origin	UK
				Origin	UK		

Go to: A063

Go to: B024

Go to: B038

Go to: A074

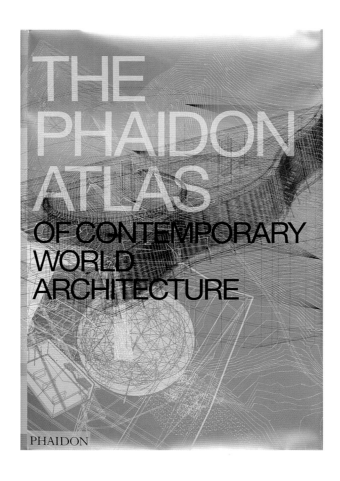

Design	**Mode**		Design	**Hamish Muir**		Design	**Multistorey**
Project	Dalton Maag		Project	The Phaidon Atlas of		Project	Mirage
	Font Book Collection_01			Contemporary World		Size	297 × 210mm
Size	240 × 170mm			Architecture			(11^{11}/$_{16}$ × 8^{53}/$_{64}$in)
	(9^{14}/$_{32}$ × 6^{3}/$_{4}$in)		Size	458 × 320mm		Pages	16
Pages	200			(18^{1}/$_{32}$ × 12^{19}/$_{32}$in)		Year	2003
Year	2004		Pages	812		Origin	UK
Origin	UK		Year	1998			
			Origin	UK			

Go to: B064–B065

Go to: A042   A060

Go to: A075

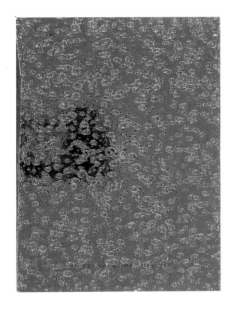

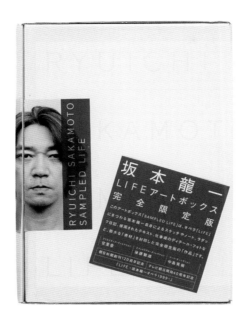

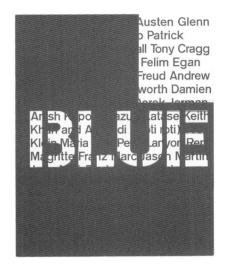

Design	**Hideki Nakajima**
Project	Revival
Size	300 × 216mm
	(11.1¹³/₁₆ × 8¹/₂in)
Pages	108
Year	1999
Origin	Japan

Design	**Hideki Nakajima**
Project	Ryuichi Sakamoto:
	Sampled Life
Size	308 × 230mm
	(12.1¹/₈ × 9³/₆₄in)
Pages	195 + other booklets
Year	1999
Origin	Japan

Design	**Michael Nash Associates**
	+ Jane
Project	Blue
Size	265 × 210mm
	(10.7¹/₁₆ × 8⁵³/₆₄in)
Pages	48
Year	2000
Origin	UK

Go to: B006

Go to: A055   B012–B013

Go to: B015

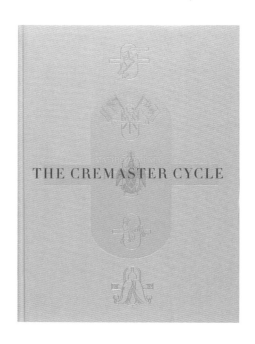

Design	**Carsten Nicolai/Olaf Bender/Jonna Groendahl**
Project	Auto Pilot: Carsten Nicolai
Size	230 × 170mm
	(9³/₆₄ × 6³/₄in)
Pages	104
Year	2002
Origin	Germany

Design	**Pentagram (Paula Scher)**
Project	Make it Bigger
Size	165 × 235mm
	(6¹/₂ × 9¹/₄in)
Pages	272
Year	2002
Origin	USA

Design	**Pentagram (J. Abbott Miller)**
Project	Matthew Barney: The Cremaster Cycle
Size	322 × 235mm
	(12¹¹/₁₆ × 9¹/₄in)
Pages	528
Year	2002
Origin	USA

Go to: A047   A073

Go to: B019

Go to: B053

Design	**Pentagram (J. Abbott Miller)**	Design	**Pentagram (J. Abbott Miller)**	Design	**Pentagram (J. Abbott Miller)**	Design

Design | **Pentagram (J. Abbott Miller)**
Project | Scanning: The Aberrant
 | Architectures of
 | Diller + Scofidio
Size | 292 × 207mm
 | (11.1¹/₂ × 8⁹/₆₄in)
Pages | 192
Year | 2003
Origin | USA

Design | **Pentagram (J. Abbott Miller)**
Project | Whitney Biennial 2000
Size | 255 × 202mm
 | (10.1¹/₃₂ × 7³¹/₃₂in)
Pages | 272
Year | 2000
Origin | USA

Design | **Pentagram (J. Abbott Miller)**
Project | Whitney Biennial 2002
Size | 255 × 205mm
 | (10.1¹/₃₂ × 8³/₃₂in)
Pages | 292
Year | 2002
Origin | USA

Design | **Ph.D**
Project | Dickson's: The Science
 | of Sensation
Size | 225 × 1.64mm
 | (8⁵⁶/₆₄ × 6²⁹/₆₄in)
Pages | 16
Year | 2004
Origin | USA

Go to: A076   B025   Go to: B054   Go to: B055   Go to: B016

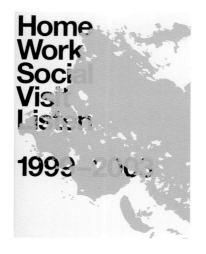

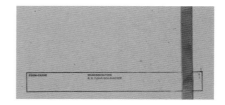

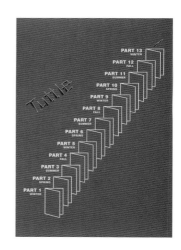

Design	**Hector Pottie**	Design	**Project M Team**	Design	**Projekttriangle**	Design	**Purtill Family Business**
Project	Home Work Social Visit	Project	Project M	Project	Form+Farbe	Project	Tuttle: In Parts, 1998–2001
	Listen 1999–2003	Size	228 × 150mm	Size	99 × 210mm	Size	241 × 166mm
Size	250 × 187mm		($8^9/_{16}$ × $5^{29}/_{32}$in)		($3^7/_8$ × $8^{53}/_{64}$in)		($9^{31}/_{64}$ × $6^{17}/_{32}$in)
	($9^{27}/_{32}$ × $7^3/_8$in)	Pages	260	Pages	26	Pages	52
Pages	60	Year	2004	Year	2000	Year	2001
Year	2004	Origin	USA	Origin	Germany	Origin	USA
Origin	UK						

Go to: B010   Go to: B026–B027   Go to: B046   Go to: B031

Design	**Rose Design**	Design	**Rose Design**	Design	**Rose Design**	Design	**Rose Design**
Project	Westzone Publishing: New Angles on Life	Project	Westzone Publishing: Preview, Spring 2001	Project	Westzone Publishing: Preview, Autumn 2001	Project	The Television Corporation: Creating Value
Size	420 × 297mm	Size	210 × 148mm	Size	148 × 116mm	Size	280 × 210mm
	(16^{17}/$_{32}$ × 11^{11}/$_{16}$in)		(8^{53}/$_{64}$ × 5^{13}/$_{16}$in)		(5^{13}/$_{16}$ × 4^{9}/$_{16}$in)		(11 × 8^{53}/$_{64}$in)
Pages	16	Pages	38	Pages	52	Pages	32
Year	2000	Year	2001	Year	2001	Year	2001
Origin	UK	Origin	UK	Origin	UK	Origin	UK

Go to: B071

Go to: B033

Go to: B075

Go to: B067

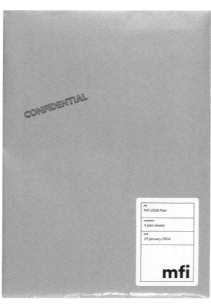

Design	Rose Design
Project	MFI, A Little Story: Summer 2003
Size	296 × 210mm (11²¹/₃₂ × 8⁵³/₆₄in)
Pages	16
Year	2003
Origin	UK

Design	Rose Design
Project	MFI 2006 Plan
Size	325 × 228mm (12⁵¹/₆₄ × 8³¹/₃₂in)
Pages	4 × folded posters
Year	2003
Origin	UK

Design	Rose Design
Project	Bodas: Cotton Basics Catalogue 2001
Size	220 × 170mm (8²¹/₃₂ × 6³/₄in)
Pages	12
Year	2001
Origin	UK

Design	Raban Ruddigkeit
Project	Freistil
Size	240 × 175mm (9⁷/₁₆ × 6⁵⁷/₆₄in)
Pages	476
Year	2003
Origin	Germany

Go to: A079

Go to: A043

Go to: B066

Go to: A076   B059

Design	**Sagmeister Inc.**
Project	Once in a Lifetime,
	Talking Heads
Size	135 × 427mm
	(5⁵/₁₆ × 1.6¹³/₁₆in)
Pages	80
Year	2003
Origin	USA

Design	**Sagmeister Inc.**
Project	Made You Look
Size	241 × 171mm
	(9³¹/₆₄ × 6⁴⁷/₆₄in)
Pages	292
Year	2001
Origin	USA

Design	**Stefan Sagmeister/**
	Anna-Maria Friedl
Project	Sagmeister: Hand Arbeit
Size	148 × 105mm
	(5¹³/₁₆ × 4⁹/₆₄in)
Pages	84
Year	2002
Origin	USA / Austria

Go to: A056

Go to: B074

Go to: B068

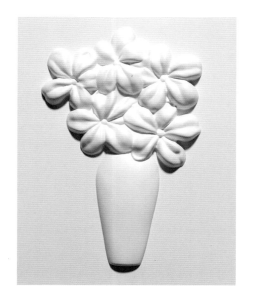

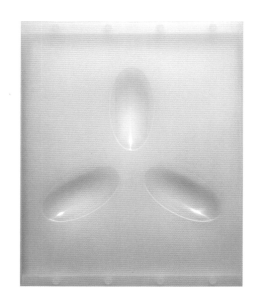

Design	**Sagmeister Inc.**
Project	Zumtobel Annual Report 01. 02
Size	271 × 21.1mm
	(1.0^{43}/$_{64}$ × 8^5/$_{16}$in)
Pages	1.1.2
Year	2003
Origin	USA

Design	**Sagmeister Inc.**
Project	Mariko Mori: Wave UFO
Size	290 × 236mm
	(1.1.^{13}/$_{32}$ × 9^{19}/$_{64}$in)
Pages	174
Year	2003
Origin	USA

Design	**Will van Sambeek**
Project	Ogenschijnlijk
Size	31.5 × 240mm
	(1.2^{13}/$_{32}$ × 9^7/$_{16}$in)
Pages	128
Year	2000
Origin	The Netherlands

Go to: A051

Go to: A050   A077

Go to: A066–A067

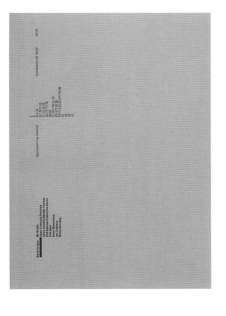

Design	**Sans + Baum**		Design	**Sans + Baum**		Design	**Robert Schäfer**	
Project	ISTD TypoGraphic 59		Project	In Sight: A Guide to Design		Project	Das Buchobjekt	
	"Back to Type"			with Low Vision in Mind		Size	249 × 148 × 70mm	
Size	297 × 213mm		Size	216 × 152mm			(9¹³/₁₆ × 5¹³/₁₆ × 2⁴⁹/₆₄in)	
	(11.⁴³/₆₄ × 8²⁵/₆₄in)			(8¹/₂ × 5³¹/₃₂in)		Pages	194	
Pages	40		Pages	2 × 152		Year	1999	
Year	2004		Year	2004		Origin	Germany	
Origin	UK		Origin	UK				

Design	**SEA Design**
Project	Wim Crouwel: Seen/Unseen
Size	264 × 209mm
	(10²⁵/₆₄ × 8¹/₄in)
Pages	32
Year	2003
Origin	UK

Go to: B029

Go to: B039

Go to: A038   B014

Go to: B017

Design	**Segura Inc.**
Project	Crop (Corbis)
Size	675 × 500mm
	(26$^{37}/_{64}$ × 1.9$^{11}/_{16}$in)
Pages	72 + 1.6 + 1.2 + 1.2
Year	2003
Origin	USA

Design	**Secondary Modern**
Project	Sandwich: A Series of
	Discursive Pamphlets
Size	148 × 105mm
	(5$^{13}/_{16}$ × 4$^{9}/_{64}$in)
Pages	Foldout poster
Year	2001
Origin	UK

Design	**Spin**
Project	Richard Artschwager:
	Up and Down/Back and Forth
Size	21.2 × 1.52mm
	(8$^{23}/_{64}$ × 5$^{31}/_{32}$in)
Pages	64
Year	2003
Origin	UK

Go to: A059

Go to: A061

Go to: A046

Droogdokkenpark Project[2]

animals

22 June – 11 September 2004
launch of version

Luther Baumgarten — 18
Berlinde de Bruyckere — 20
Katharina Fritsch — 22
Ellen Gallagher — 24
John Isaacs — 26
Marnie Kappes — 28
Mike Kelley — 30
Oswaldo Macià — 32
Jean-Luc Mylayne — 34
Bruce Nauman — 36
João Onofre — 38
Marjetica Potrč — 40
Mejan Cartwolt — 42
Kiki Smith — 44
Diana Thater — 46
Rosemarie Trockel — 48
Bill Viola — 50

||/

onedotzero
motion blur

graphic moving imagemakers

dvd

book

Design	**Spin**	Design	**Spin**	Design	**State**
Project	Droogdokkenpark: Project[2]	Project	Animals	Project	Motion Blur, OneDotZero
Size	301 × 305mm	Size	277 × 204mm	Size	320 × 253mm
	(11.27/32 × 12in)		(10.7/8 × 8in)		(12.19/32 × 9.9/16in)
Pages	24 + 34	Pages	72	Pages	232
Year	2002	Year	2004	Year	2004
Origin	UK	Origin	UK	Origin	UK

Go to: B048

Go to: A062

Go to: A045

Design	**Struktur Design**
Project	Magalogue.4 (Alamy)
Size	250 × 250mm
	(9²⁷/₃₂ × 9²⁷/₃₂in)
Pages	52
Year	2004
Origin	UK/Denmark

Design	**Struktur Design**
Project	Alamy–Two Sides to Every Story
Size	297 × 105mm
	(11¹¹/₁₆ × 4⁹/₆₄in)
Pages	2 × 32
Year	2002
Origin	UK

Design	**Struktur Design**
Project	Minutes
Size	223 × 164mm
	(8²⁵/₃₂ × 6²⁹/₆₄in)
Pages	36
Year	2002
Origin	UK

Go to: B055
Go to: A060–A061
Go to: B032

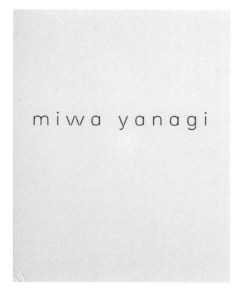

miwa yanagi

Design	**Surface/Miwa Yanagi**	Design	**Underware /Piet Schreuders**
Project	Miwa Yanagi	Project	Read Naked
Size	302 × 230mm	Size	205 × 184mm
	(11.7/8 × 9.3/64in)		(8.3/32 × 7.1/4in)
Pages	44 + 78	Pages	48
Year	2004	Year	2002
Origin	Germany/Japan	Origin	The Netherlands

Go to: B056–B057

Go to: B018

A024/
kagir

Design	**Robert Schäfer**
Project	Das Buchobjekt
Size	249 × 148 × 70mm
	(9¹³/₁₆ × 5¹³/₁₆ × 2⁴⁹/₆₄in)
Pages	194
Year	1999
Origin	Germany

The designer/author of this beautiful work has considered every aspect of the project. The book comes packaged inside a specially made, white, corrugated cardboard box. This acts as an integral part of the overall work, with title information printed in black and red. Once opened, the book is revealed cradled within a nest of shredded paper offcuts—this is, in fact, the trimmed waste from the book's own production.

Go to: B014

Design	**Fabrica**
Project	Mail Me
Size	250 × 1.57 × 95mm
	(9^{27}/$_{32}$ × 6^3/$_{16}$ × 3^3/$_4$in)
Pages	160 + 320
Year	2003
Origin	Italy

With e-mail now being the prime form of communication for most people across the globe, Fabrica decided to create a project that celebrated the diversity of postal-based design. Designers from around the world sent in postcards on the theme of "mail me," with contributors including Alan Fletcher, Ed Fella, and Uwe Loesch. Two books were produced, the first containing an introduction to the project, and images of all 106 postcards , and the second containing the actual postcards, simply bound with a glued spine, allowing the cards to be easily removed and posted. The two books are beautifully contained within a custom-made, thick cardboard box. The packaging offers more than just protection—it forms the true cover of the piece. Without this outer cover, the books would lose meaning.

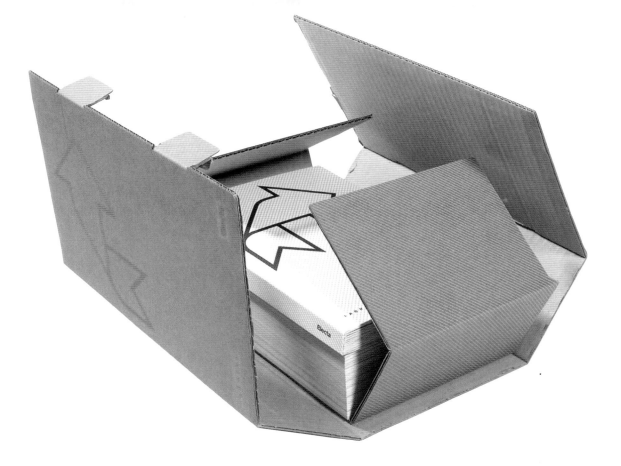

Go to: A040   B028

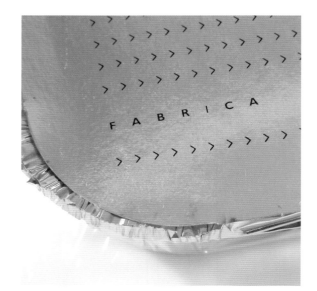

Design	**Fabrica**
Project	2398 gr.: A Book About Food
Size	280 × 222mm
	(11 × 8¾in)
Pages	320
Year	2003
Origin	Italy

Produced by Fabrica, the research and communication center of Italian clothing company Benetton. The book is based around the general concept "food for thought" and focuses on all aspects of food and the consumption of it. The title, 2398 gr., is a reference to the actual weight of the book naked—no packaging.

A limited edition—only available in the chicest boutiques of Paris and Milan—used a specially created ceramic plate to house the book. It is now highly collectable. The edition shown here, produced in much larger quantities and available worldwide, still had very distinctive packaging—an off-the-shelf, take-out tinfoil box. The book fits neatly inside, and the result is a total package that instantly reflects the book's content, that stands out dramatically from everything else in a bookshop, and that is cost-effective.

Go to: A039   B028

Design	**Irma Boom**
Project	Gutenberg-Galaxie II
Size	290 × 193mm
	(11.13/32 × 719/32in)
Pages	2 × 208
Year	2002
Origin	The Netherlands

Designed by Irma Boom and featuring a vast selection of her award-winning work, this book was commissioned by the city of Leipzig, Germany, as a celebration of her outstanding contribution to book design.

The book comes wrapped in a sheet of brown paper with a diagram of the galaxy printed in magenta and lime green. Within its brown packaging, the book feels like a standard portrait-format, case-bound book. However, when the wrappings have been removed, the true format of the book is unveiled. The book is formed by two volumes, one above the other, or, if you prefer, one portrait book that has been sliced in half through to the paper of the back cover. This acts as a hinge, allowing the two sections to fold precisely in half. Once folded, the book works equally well as a small, landscape-format book .

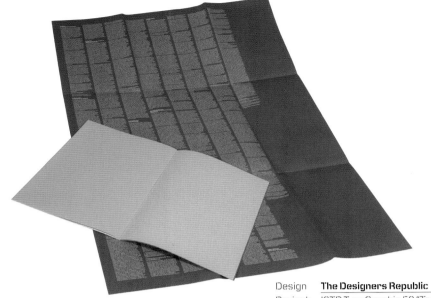

Design	**The Designers Republic**
Project	ISTD TypoGraphic 58 "Too Much Noise Not Enough Time"
Size	310 × 223mm
	(12.13/64 × 825/32in)
Pages	32
Year	2002
Origin	UK

Each issue of this journal for the International Society of Typographic Designers features a guest designer. The single constant is the format of the journal; with this one given, the designers are allowed to do as they see fit. With this issue, The Designers Republic maintained a conventional saddle stitched, 32-page journal with standard 4-page cover. However, the journal has no text or images in it whatsoever—the plain, mid-tone gray cover is opened to reveal a spectrum of vibrant full-bleed colors running spread after spread.

The manuscript for the entire journal is printed onto a large sheet of gray paper which is used to wrap it, turning this disposable packaging into precious content. The journal itself becomes a beautiful series of color-fields. The metaphors are left open to interpretation, although the subtitle, "Too Much Noise Not Enough Time," could be a clue.

Go to: B011   B042–B043 B069   B070

Go to: A065

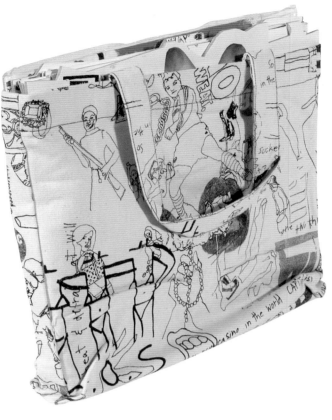

Design	**Chicks on Speed**
Project	It's a Project
Size	325 × 265mm
	(12^{51}/$_{64}$ × 10^{7}/$_{16}$in)
Pages	228
Year	2004
Origin	USA

The art scene trio Chicks on Speed extend their highly original style into every aspect of this book, which is both by them and about them. The assembled elements of this package come shrink-wrapped in order to give structure to the spontaneous nature of the work. The package contains a useful bag in which all the fragments can be held. Along with the book and cloth bag comes a dressmaker's pattern for a set of overalls, a unisex dress, a CD of Chicks on Speed's music, and a poster. The package covers all the diverse aspects of the team's work—music, art, fashion, and everything in between.

Design	**Hamish Muir**
Project	The Phaidon Atlas of
	Contemporary World
	Architecture
Size	458 × 320mm
	(18^{1}/$_{32}$ × 12^{19}/$_{32}$in)
Pages	812
Year	1998
Origin	UK

This huge architecture book, vast in both scale and weight, is contained within a special, clear plastic case, the design of which aids its transport. Weighing over 17¼lb (8kg), the book's physical size helps to convey the scale of the information held within its 800-plus pages—it features over 1,000 architectural projects from every corner of the world.

The case has a comfortable handle and is sturdy enough to protect its weighty contents.

Go to: A057   B057   Go to: A060

Design	**Rose Design**
Project	MFI 2006 Plan
Size	325 × 228mm
	(12.51/64 × 8.31/32in)
Pages	4 × folded posters
Year	2003
Origin	UK

For an internal staff conference of
the British furniture superstore MFI,
the designers took a very different
approach to the standard sales report
format. The focus of the conference
was the future plans and development
of the company. Adopting this as their
theme, the designers used the visual
pun of a series of blueprints which
opened out to reveal plans for a
residential housing development, and
floor plans for a house, focusing on
the rooms that the company as a whole
provides furniture for. These plans are
contained in a plain manila envelope,
marked confidential, that was handed
out at the conference inside an
anonymous, brown-paper bag.

Go to: A079   B033   B066   B067   B071.   B075

Design	**Dowling Design**
Project	Simon Patterson
	Colour Match screensaver
Size	Ø 1.90mm
	(7³¹/₆₄in)
Pages	24
Year	2001
Origin	UK

The packaging of this CD and booklet for the artist Simon Patterson is the most visually striking aspect of this conceptual audiovisual project, commissioned by Tate Enterprises. The high-density foam ball comes in a string net with the booklet attached; the CD is concealed in a slot in the ball.

The project forms the third part of a series of works begun in 1997. The CD contains a screen saver featuring the voice of John Cavanagh, a radio presenter for BBC Scotland, best known for announcing the football (soccer) results. He recites the name of every team that has ever played in the Scottish Football League, along with a goal score versus the reference number for a Pantone printing color. The on-screen monitor changes color in line with Cavanagh's results.

Design	**David James Associates**
Project	The Order of Things
Size	185 × 260mm
	(7⁹/₃₂ × 10¹⁵/₆₄in)
Pages	176
Year	2001
Origin	UK

The general perception of what a book should be is completely destroyed by this very original solution to a fashion photography design. The book is without beginning, end, or spine, and there is no front or back cover, immediately turning the book into an object in its own right. It has instant showstopping appeal and quite literally stands out in any bookshop. Housed in a clear plastic drum to show off its unique format, all information about the project is applied to a black sticker on the drum's side.

Go to: B061

Design	**State**
Project	Motion Blur, OneDotZero
Size	320 × 253mm
	(12^{19}/$_{32}$ × 9^{9}/$_{16}$in)
Pages	232
Year	2004
Origin	UK

Housed within a custom-built slipcase of black, high-density foam, which echoes the stealth look of the Sony PlayStation, this book and DVD of new media work has a dramatic and impactive presence. The title is laser cut into the foam to reveal fragments of the book's cover. The laser-cut typography contrasts with the other type, which is screen printed, in white ink, on the foam's surface. The slipcase features two slots, one for the book and a second to hold the DVD in place. The elaborate nature of the slipcase makes this packaging an indispensable element of the book.

Design	**Atelier Roger Pfund**
Project	Hundert T Variationen
Size	230 × 1.70mm
	(9^{1}/$_{16}$ × 6^{3}/$_{4}$in)
Pages	240
Year	2000
Origin	Germany

Reminiscent of an old cigar box, this highly unusual top-loading slipcase creates a striking and eclectic taster for the book itself. Slipping the book out of its wooden case reveals a plain blue cover with an uppercase T die cut to reveal the black endpapers beneath. The book shows the different responses to the letter T from 100 designers around the world.

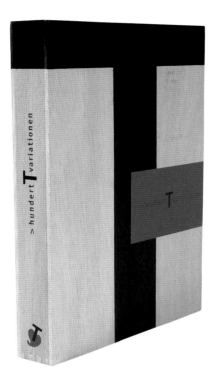

Design	**Spin**
Project	Richard Artschwager: Up and Down/Back and Forth
Size	21.2 × 1.52mm
	(8^{23}/$_{64}$ × 5^{31}/$_{32}$in)
Pages	64
Year	2003
Origin	UK

This simple A5 (5^{3}/$_{4}$ × 8^{1}/$_{4}$in) catalog, for an exhibition of artist Richard Artschwager's charcoal drawings, is housed within a sturdy slipcase. Although simple, the production values of this piece help to unite the catalog with the artist's sculptural works— Artschwager is known for his use of wood-effect plastic laminates. These laminates are echoed in the slipcase. The catalog fits snugly inside the case and forms a solid mass; again, such precision and solidity are qualities in the artist's work. The high-gloss, hard surfaces of the exterior are replaced with soft, uncoated paper within the catalog, echoing the feel of the charcoal drawings illustrated.

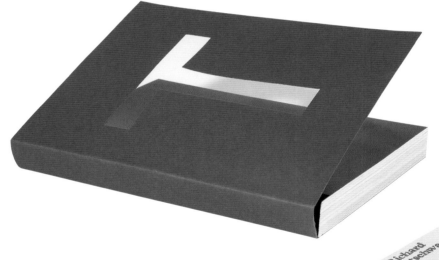

Go to: A062 B048

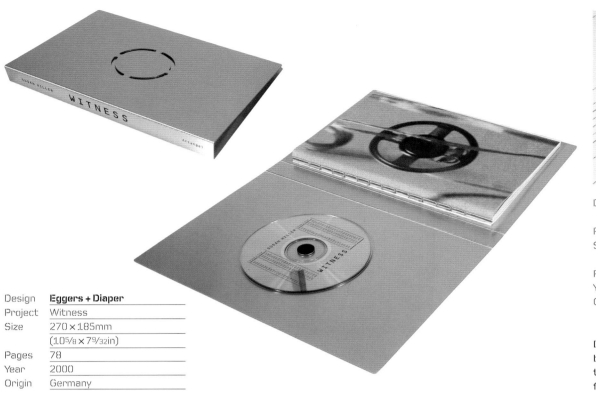

Design	**Eggers + Diaper**
Project	Witness
Size	270 × 185mm
	(10⁵/8 × 7⁹/32in)
Pages	78
Year	2000
Origin	Germany

This book and CD were produced to accompany an installation by the artist Susan Hiller, which featured a room filled with small loudspeakers hung from the ceiling by their own cables. Each speaker played a different sound recording of a witness to an extraterrestrial experience. The book features transcripts from these, together with various preliminary drawings and photographs by Hiller.

The cover is made from aluminum with some circular, die-cut slits in the front. These slits reveal the surface of a CD that is attached to the inside front cover. The slits are inspired by the shape of the loudspeakers used in the installation.

The book itself is smaller than the metal covers and is bonded to the inside back cover only; this allows it to be read unhindered by the ridged covers. The spine of the book is left uncovered, leaving the "guts" of the binding method visible.

Design	**Carsten Nicolai/Olaf Bender/Jonna Groendahl**
Project	Auto Pilot: Carsten Nicolai
Size	230 × 170mm
	(9³/64 × 6³/4in)
Pages	104
Year	2002
Origin	Germany

Dispatched in a clear, resealable plastic bag printed in white, this book about the artist, musician, and record label founder Carsten Nicolai shows a close affinity with his audio and visual projects: these use vast quantities of white, with a light and discreet use of typography. The book includes a CD of his audio work, which is cleverly housed within the gatefolded front cover. A die-cut circle in this cover reveals the central spine and a small circle of yellow, the only bright color used in the piece.

Go to: A070   B008

Go to: A073

Design	**Experimental Jetset**
Project	The People's Art
Size	185 × 127mm
	(7⁹/₃₂ × 5in)
Pages	128
Year	2001
Origin	The Netherlands

Ten different dust jackets, each featuring the work of one of the featured contributors, are used to wrap this catalog. The physical bulk of these covers adds weight and substance to the project. They are also the only visual element—the catalog itself is text only, printed in red and black. This democratic method allows each artist the honor of a cover image. The book is held together with a belly band that includes the title of the project and a list of the contributors.

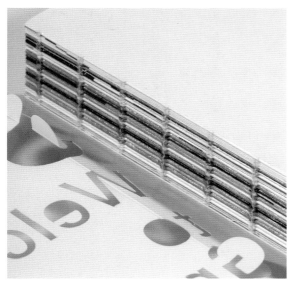

Design	**Benzin**
Project	Super: Welcome to Graphic Wonderland
Size	240 × 166mm
	(9⁷⁄₁₆ × 6¹⁷⁄₃₂in)
Pages	412
Year	2003
Origin	Switzerland

The usual job description for a dust jacket is "protect your precious contents," however, with this book of cutting-edge graphic design it is the dust jacket that needs protecting. The letterforms of the book's title have been die cut from the fluorescent yellow card. The die-cut letters extend around onto the spine, and while this increases the fragility of the cover it also, in pushing the concept so far, instills a sense of awe. As the book has no additional cover, the binding of the sewn sections is exposed in all its natural beauty.

Design	**Sagmeister Inc.**
Project	Mariko Mori: Wave UFO
Size	290 × 236mm
	(11.^{13}/$_{32}$ × 9.^{19}/$_{64}$in)
Pages	174
Year	2003
Origin	USA

Wave UFO is enshrouded in a white, translucent slipcase of polypropylene. Such a minimal introduction sets the stage for the rest of this book about Japanese artist Mariko Mori, renowned for her love of all things space-age and alien.

The slipcase has three sculpted indents in both the front and back covers and the matte surface of the slipcase contrasts with these shiny recesses. They provide the only motif on the surface, and form an abstract symbol for the artist. They also hold the book firmly in position inside the large case. As the book is 16mm (^{1}/$_{16}$in) and the slipcase 40mm (1.^{1}/$_{2}$in) thick, this gives the impression that the book is suspended in space.

The translucent plastic partly reveals the subtle morphic color of the book held within, and this focuses the attention on the book's spine on which the full spectrum of morphic color is revealed for the first time. The title of the project is embossed on the spine, and this is echoed on the spine of the slipcase.

Go to: A051   A056   A077   B068   B074

Design	**Sagmeister Inc.**
Project	Zumtobel Annual Report 01 02
Size	271 × 211mm
	(10 43/64 × 8 5/16 in)
Pages	112
Year	2003
Origin	USA

The cover of this annual report for the
lighting company Zumtobel features
special plastic extrusions on both the
front and the back. The front cover has
a vase of flowers and the back, the title
of the report. The "still life" image on
the front is used within the book as
a subject to showcase the various
special lighting effects that the
company is capable of.

The uncovered spine holds
the company name which is formed by
printing small fragments of the type
on each of the folded sections of the
report; once bound together, these
fragments align to form the words.

Inside, the clean and
structured typography of the report
is contrasted with the vibrant and
dramatic effects of the photography.

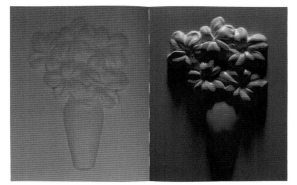

Go to: A050   A056   A077   B068   B074

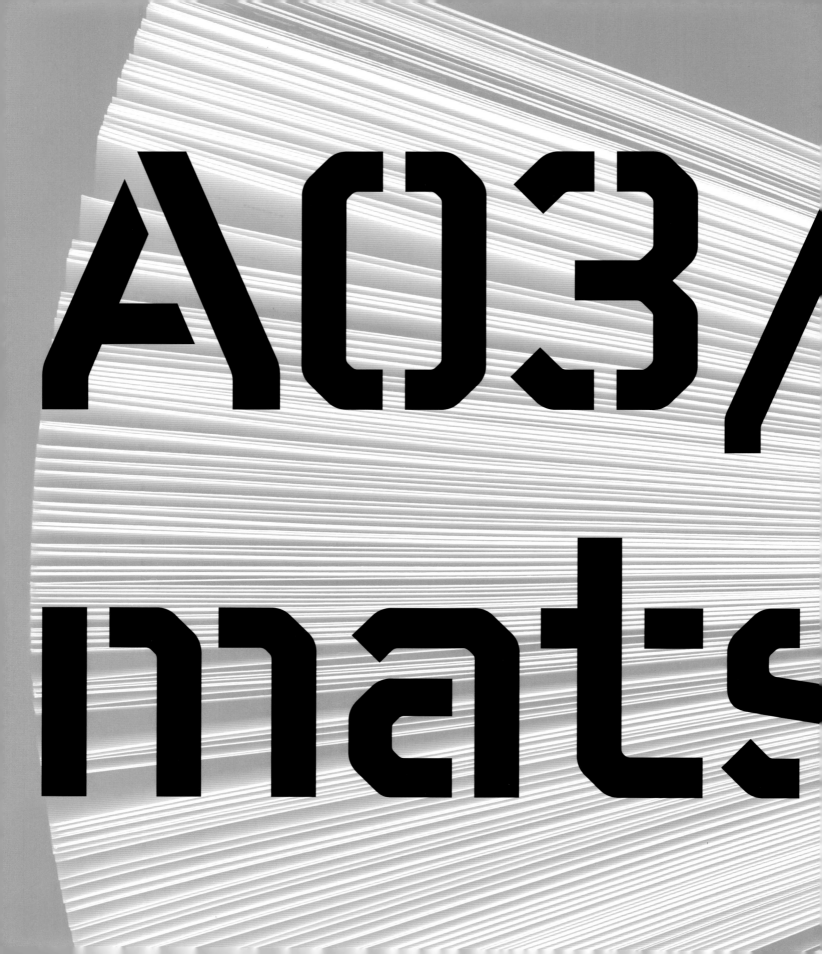

For

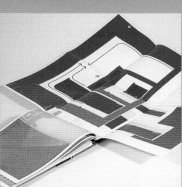

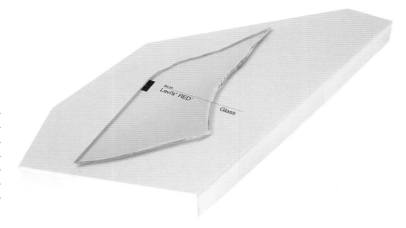

Design	**The Kitchen**
Project	Levi's Red: Glass
Size	280 × 138mm
	(11 × 5⁷/₁₆in)
Pages	20
Year	2001
Origin	UK

This promotional fashion brochure for Levi's plays graphically with the title of the collection—Red Glass. The irregular-shaped box it is housed in echoes the photograph of a shard of glass that is printed on its lid. The lid is removed to reveal nine individual 3mm-(¹⁄₈in) thick sheets of board, all cut to the same irregular shape. The designers have continued this experimental direction in the layout of information. With such a nonstandard format, a conventional grid is futile, however, they have maintained a consistent use of typography and photography. Although positioned differently on every board, the images all bleed off the edge and wrap around onto the reverse. This breaks the otherwise standard format of the rectangular image boxes, allowing thin fragments of image to splinter across. The fashion photography continues the glass theme, with models smashing fists through car windows and kicking out the glass from bus shelters.

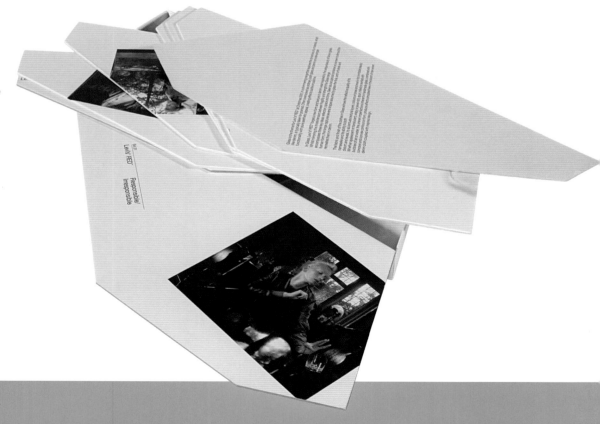

Design	**Hideki Nakajima**
Project	Ryuichi Sakamoto: Sampled Life
Size	308 × 230mm
	(12¹⁄₈ × 9³⁄₆₄in)
Pages	195 + other booklets
Year	1999
Origin	Japan

This package was produced to accompany Japanese composer Ryuichi Sakamoto's opera Life. It is comprised of four books and various loose-leaf elements, all housed within a special cardboard box.

The title of the work is overprinted in white on the white surface of the box, establishing a minimal color code that continues throughout. The box is sealed with a sticker, printed in black-and-red, with a portrait of the composer. The inside of the box is printed with extracts of text in gray, in both Japanese and English.

Go to: B006   B012–B013

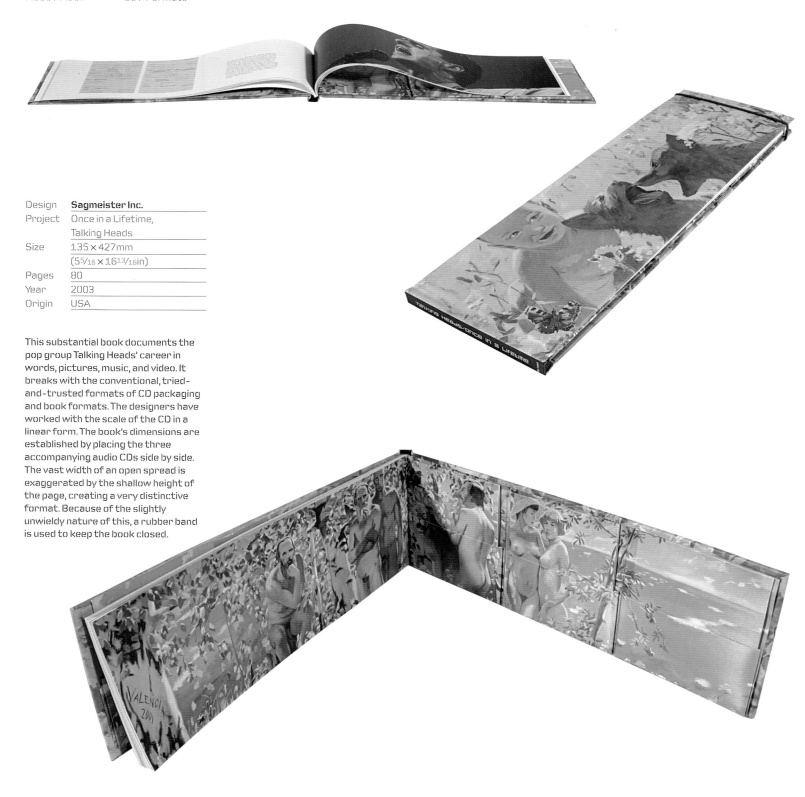

Design	**Sagmeister Inc.**
Project	Once in a Lifetime, Talking Heads
Size	135 × 427mm (5⁵/₁₆ × 16¹³/₁₆in)
Pages	80
Year	2003
Origin	USA

This substantial book documents the pop group Talking Heads' career in words, pictures, music, and video. It breaks with the conventional, tried-and-trusted formats of CD packaging and book formats. The designers have worked with the scale of the CD in a linear form. The book's dimensions are established by placing the three accompanying audio CDs side by side. The vast width of an open spread is exaggerated by the shallow height of the page, creating a very distinctive format. Because of the slightly unwieldy nature of this, a rubber band is used to keep the book closed.

Go to: A050   A051   A077   B068   B074

Design	**Chicks on Speed**
Project	It's a Project
Size	325 × 265mm
	(12$^{51}/_{64}$ × 10$^7/_{16}$in)
Pages	228
Year	2004
Origin	USA

The spontaneous nature of Chicks on Speed's work is echoed in the chaotic style of this book. The book itself gives the impression of a handmade scrapbook, with each section a different size and shape from the one before. The cover exaggerates this effect—it is an irregular shape and has various jagged angles seemingly hacked out of it. The fact that this is a mass-produced book and not a one-off artist's book make the overall effect even more impressive.

Go to: A042   B057

Design	FL@33
Project	Trans-form
Size	497 × 320mm
	(19^{37}/$_{64}$ × 12^{19}/$_{32}$in)
Pages	32
Year	2001
Origin	UK

Produced as a special magazine-style project, the work shown in this piece is all based around a series of images of cranes and the construction process. The large scale of the project helps to create dramatic contrasts from spread to spread. The inclusion of a CD, housed in a clear plastic wallet that is bound into the spine, reinforces this contrast of scale.

Go to: B037

Design	**Segura Inc.**
Project	Crop (Corbis)
Size	675 × 500mm
	($26^{37}/_{64}$ × $1.9^{11}/_{16}$in)
Pages	72 + 1.6 + 1.2 + 1.2
Year	2003
Origin	USA

The vast scale of this picture library catalog is such that it was distributed rolled up in a tube. With the exception of a very small booklet of portraits (below), the catalog is left unbound. The loose feel this gives works well over such a large expanse of printed sheet. The piece cannot be flicked through as would be the norm for such a catalog: the scale demands a large, clear desk and some time to turn the huge pages. The designers have used the selected images to dramatic effect. Different categories of the library's collection are contained within various supplements that work against the larger backdrop of the main catalog.

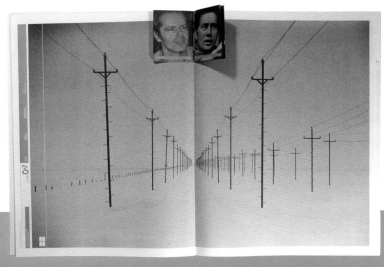

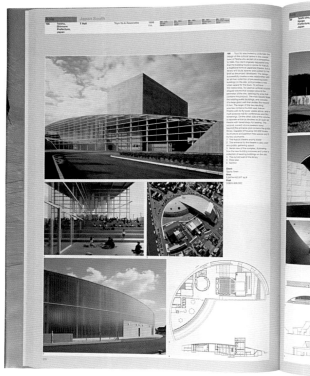

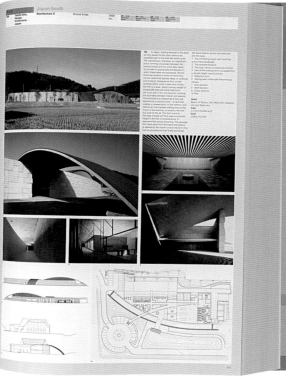

Design	**Hamish Muir**
Project	The Phaidon Atlas of Contemporary World Architecture
Size	458 × 320mm
	(18$^{1/32}$ × 12$^{19/32}$in)
Pages	812
Year	1998
Origin	UK

The sheer size and weight of this book sets it apart from any other architecture book available. This is both a blessing and a curse: in the bookshop it cannot help but get noticed, but once purchased and transported home, the book is too large for any bookshelf.

Go to: A042

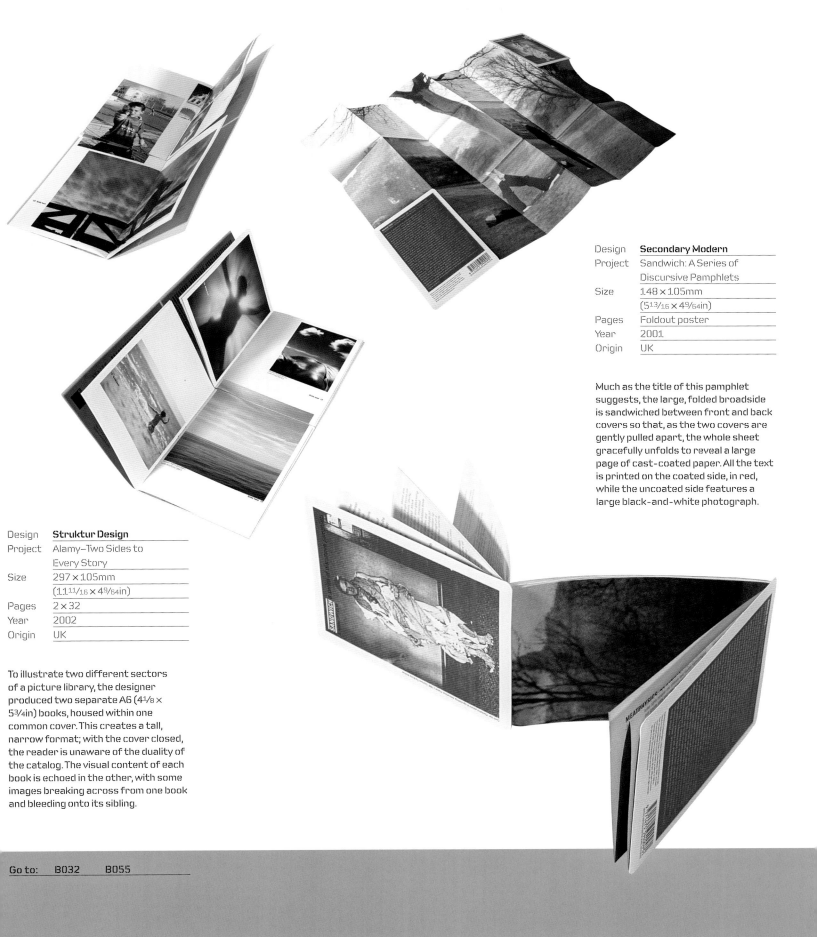

Design	**Secondary Modern**
Project	Sandwich: A Series of
	Discursive Pamphlets
Size	148 × 105mm
	(5¹³/₁₆ × 4⁹/₆₄in)
Pages	Foldout poster
Year	2001
Origin	UK

Much as the title of this pamphlet suggests, the large, folded broadside is sandwiched between front and back covers so that, as the two covers are gently pulled apart, the whole sheet gracefully unfolds to reveal a large page of cast-coated paper. All the text is printed on the coated side, in red, while the uncoated side features a large black-and-white photograph.

Design	**Struktur Design**
Project	Alamy—Two Sides to
	Every Story
Size	297 × 105mm
	(11.¹¹/₁₆ × 4⁹/₆₄in)
Pages	2 × 32
Year	2002
Origin	UK

To illustrate two different sectors of a picture library, the designer produced two separate A6 (4¹/₈ × 5³/₄in) books, housed within one common cover. This creates a tall, narrow format; with the cover closed, the reader is unaware of the duality of the catalog. The visual content of each book is echoed in the other, with some images breaking across from one book and bleeding onto its sibling.

Go to: B032   B055

Design	**Spin**
Project	Animals
Size	277 × 204mm
	(10⁷/8 × 8in)
Pages	72
Year	2004
Origin	UK

There is nothing particularly unusual about the outside of this art catalog for a group show at the Haunch of Venison gallery in London. However, the introductory essays, printed on a gray, uncoated stock, have been scaled down in proportion to the rest of the catalog, forming a smaller book within a book. This creates a great contrast, both in size and material, to the main image section which is printed on a coated stock. The back section of the catalog is also printed on the gray stock. It uses full-size pages, but the text occupies the same scaled-down page area as the introductory section.

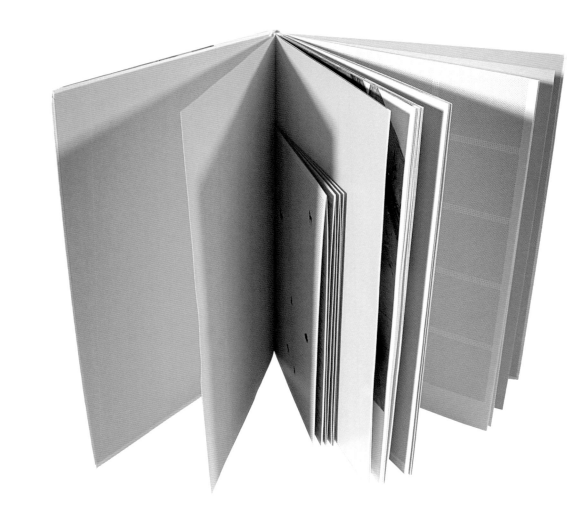

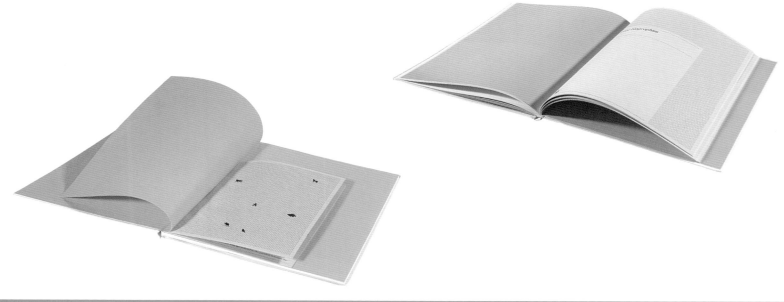

Go to: A046   B048

"Why do we define space with fences? Why don't we take our litter home? Why do we think we can survive without beauty?"
Sir Ian McKellen, Actor

cabe space

"It's easy to become blind to wasted space—you don't even notice it as you pass by every day. But imagine if this space was a fantastic park where you could sit during the day and watch kids playing football and at night come to live music events."
Trevor Nelson MBE
Broadcaster/presenter

How many times do people walk past neglected council estates, rundown playgrounds, disused car parks or other forgotten patches without even noticing them?

With over two million households suffering significant rubbish in the areas where they live and 1.5 million households troubled by graffiti and vandalism, it is no wonder that the Government has put improving quality of life high on its urban agenda. The Wasted Space? campaign is a new initiative by CABE Space, the recently formed unit at the Commission for Architecture and the Built Environment (CABE). The campaign will aim to help local people draw attention to land that is sadly going to waste and blighting their local environment.

People want to live in communities with a range of well maintained public spaces—parks, community gardens, places for wildlife, places for children to play, places where you can simply sit and watch the world go by or meet a friend for a chat. "I find it hard to think of many examples of public spaces created during the past 50 years which have that feel-good factor. We are the fourth-wealthiest nation in the world, and yet we have chosen for a long time to dress ourselves in rags", says Sir Stuart Lipton, CABE's chairman.

Instead of continuing to build ourselves a nation dressed in rags, Lipton implores us to take a look around, spot those wasted spaces, enhance and hold them up as civic mirrors, to reflect the ambition and aspiration of the local community. "Let us build a nation that exhibits its riches in its shared environment, that wears its pride on its sleeve", adds Lipton.

CABE Space

cabe space

Design	**Made Thought**
Project	Wasted Space?
Size	265 × 190mm
	(10⁷/₁₆ × 7³¹/₆₄in)
Pages	24
Year	2002
Origin	UK

This report on the reclamation of wasteland in England plays with format visually. An eight-page color section, printed on coated stock, is wrapped around a larger brochure of uncoated stock, a visual reference to the wasted space that extends throughout the brochure. The text pages occupy this same small format; the surrounding area is filled by images of wasteland. In the latter pages of the report, images illustrate both how this wasteland can be utilized, and the resultant benefits to the community.

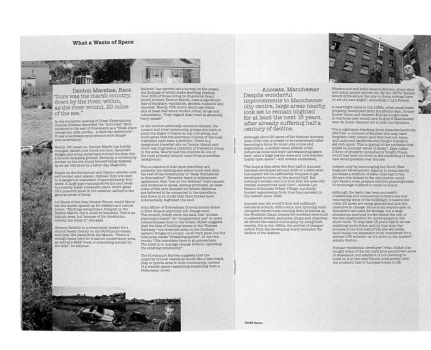

What a Waste of Space

Denton Marshes, Kent
"Ours was the marsh country, down by the river, within, as the river wound, 20 miles of the sea."

In the evocative opening of Great Expectations, Charles Dickens described the "shrouded" Kent marshes to the east of Gravesend as a "bleak place overgrown with nettles... a dark flat wilderness". It was a landscape synonymous with danger and uncertainty.

Nearly 180 years on, Denton Marsh has hardly changed, except now burnt-out cars, discarded fridges and scrap metal have turned the area into a derelict dumping ground. Recently, a community worker on the site found himself being targeted by an air rifle fired by a latter-day Magwitch.

People on the Northcourt and Denton estates need well-tended open spaces. Instead, they live next to a dangerous wasteland of approximately four acres. A large pipe running above the land leads to a nearby water treatment plant, which gives off a powerful smell in hot weather; adding to the general sense of decay.

Liz Sharp of the local Denton Forum would like to see the marsh opened up for walkers and nature lovers. "Stuff has always been dumped on the Denton Marsh, but it could be beautiful. This is an historic area, but because of the dereliction, nobody can enjoy it", she says.

Graeme Baldwin is a community worker for a church-based charity on the Northcourt estate, and lives 100 yards from the Marsh. "There is enough spare here for a nature conservancy area, as well as a BMX track or something similar for the kids", he believes.

Baldwin has carried out a survey on the estate, the findings of which make startling reading. Over 80% of those living on Shamrock Road, which borders Denton Marsh, have a significant fear of burglary, vandalism, general nuisance and disorder. Nearly 70% worry about car crime and at least half about violent crime, drugs and intimidation. They regard their road as generally "very unsafe".

In the current politically sensitive climate, the council and local community groups are loath to point the finger of blame at any one group, but most agree that the activities of some of the local travellers have been a problem. There is a designated traveller site on Denton Marsh and there has long been a tradition of travellers living in the area. Nearly half the children at one of the local primary schools come from a traveller background.

The consensus is that most travellers are perfectly law abiding and either work well with the rest of the community or "keep themselves to themselves". However, there is widespread agreement that "one or two families" have caused, and continue to cause, serious problems. At least some of the cars dumped on Denton Marshes are believed to be connected to the travellers, and there is no doubt that their horses have substantially degraded the land.

John Miller of Gravesham Council admits there is little chance anything will change soon. The council, which owns the land, has "outline planning consent" for "employment use" at some indeterminate time in the future. Miller suggests that the idea of building homes in the Thames Gateway—the riverside area on the furthest eastern fringes of London—is all very good, but the local area needs "breathing spaces", in his own words. "The travellers have to go somewhere. The trick is to manage change without upsetting the existing community".

The Northcourt Survey suggests that the majority of local residents would like a bike track, play or sports area in their community, instead of a wasted space resembling something from a Dickensian novel.

Ancoats, Manchester
Despite wonderful improvements to Manchester city centre, large areas nearby look set to remain blighted for at least the next 15 years, after already suffering half a century of decline.

Although about 20 acres of the historic Ancoats area of the city is poised to be redeveloped after becoming a focus for inner-city crime and deprivation, a similar-sized swathe of old industrial units and their accompanying spare land—plus a large barren area and now-derelict "public open space"—will remain untouched.

"The hope is that after the first half of Ancoats becomes developed around 2015 or a little later, the market will be sufficiently buoyant to get developers to move on the second half. But nothing's certain and it is true that the area will remain unimproved until then", admits Lyn Fenton of Ancoats Urban Village, a publicly-funded regeneration body that has operated in the district since 1996.

Ancoats was the world's first self-sufficient industrial suburb, with cotton and spinning mills alongside warehouses sending their products up the Rochdale Canal; houses for workers were built in adjacent streets, and pubs, shops and churches all served the textile community by being built nearby. But in the 1850s, the arrival of cheaper cotton from the developing world heralded the decline of the district.

Warehouses and mills became derelict, shops shut and many people moved out. By the 1970s "people would drive across the city to dump rubbish here or set old cars alight", according to Lyn Fenton.

A new blight came in the 1980s, when small-scale property developers from the Middle East, former Soviet Union and western Europe bought sites in the hope they would turn to gold if Manchester won its much-vaunted bid to host the Olympics.

"It's a nightmare tracking down absentee landlords like this—a mixture of families who may have forgotten they owned land that had lost value, and unknown landlords who bought hoping to get rich quick. This is typical of the problems that added to Ancoats' sense of decay", says Julian D'Arcy of property consultancy Knight Frank, which has been involved in the marketing of some new developments near the site.

Indeed, only by encouraging the North West Regional Development Agency to compulsorily purchase a mixture of sites—that half of the 40 acres site closest to the city centre—could Lyn Fenton even prepare the first planning briefs to encourage builders to come on board.

Although the tactic has been successful (residential and commercial builders are now renovating some of the buildings), it means the other 20 acres are being ignored and lack the incentive to change. Some small warehouses on this sector are used for storage, but a large abandoned smelting works makes the rest of the site unattractive for development in the short term. "It may take 15 years before we see anything move there, and by that time the success of the first half of the site will make land values too expensive to be considered for a similar CPO scheme—so it's down to the market", admits Fenton.

Popular residential developer Urban Splash has bought some of the old units plus around two acres of wasteland, but admits it is not planning to build on it in the near future, presumably until the southern half of Ancoats comes to life.

CABE Space

Go to: B024   B038

Design	**Base Design**
Project	Women'secret
	Look Book: Automne 03
Size	210 × 152mm
	(8⁵³/₆₄ × 5³¹/₃₂in)
Pages	6 × folded posters
Year	2003
Origin	Spain/Belgium/USA

This four-leafed folder opens to reveal a series of six separate folded sheets, each shot by a different photographer. The sheets are thin, cast-coated stock; the high-gloss side is used for the images while the uncoated reverse is left blank. The physical nature of these sheets prevents the reader from flicking through the pages in a conventional manner.

Go to: B036   B044   B051

Design	**The Designers Republic**
Project	3D→2D: Adventures in and out of Architecture
Size	230 × 340mm (9³/₆₄ × 13²⁵/₆₄in)
Pages	198
Year	2000
Origin	UK

Thinly veiled as a book on architecture, this project forms the perfect platform for the designers to play with their own distinctive graphic language. The large, wire-bound, landscape format contains numerous half-width pages printed on different stock to hide and reveal images and type, plus various gatefolds and large-format foldout posters. Typographic direction for the reader appears throughout the book, "overloading" the information required to navigate its pages.

Go to: A041

Design	**Will van Sambeek**
Project	Ogenschijnlijk
Size	315 × 240mm
	(1.2¹³/₃₂ × 9⁷/₁₆in)
Pages	128
Year	2000
Origin	The Netherlands

This lavish book features foldouts on virtually every spread. The visual richness reaches a climax with this elaborate section in which the large-format pages unfold to reveal the epic ceiling painting <u>Glorification of Saint Ignatius</u> (1691.–1694), by Andrea Pozzo. As easily as they open, they obediently fold back down again. Visual tricks and codes are used throughout the book, including stereo 3-D imaging (complete with red/green glasses).

The visual tricks are even extended to the book's packaging; it comes inside a white cardboard casing with the cover partially printed in such a way as to appear that the outer casing is being ripped off the book.

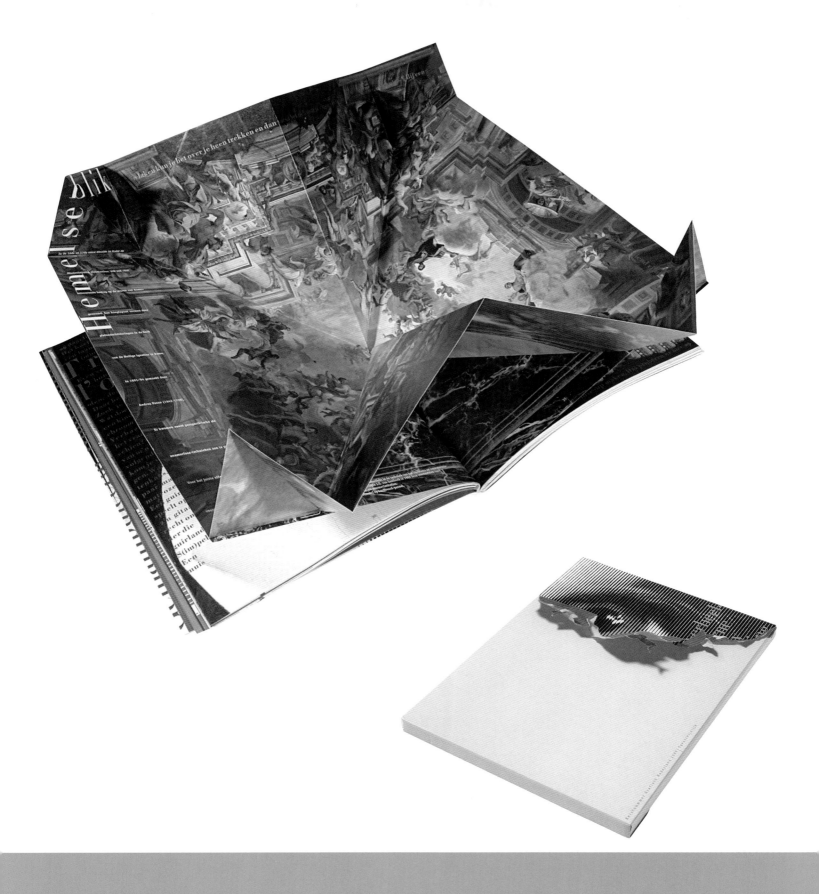

A04/erial

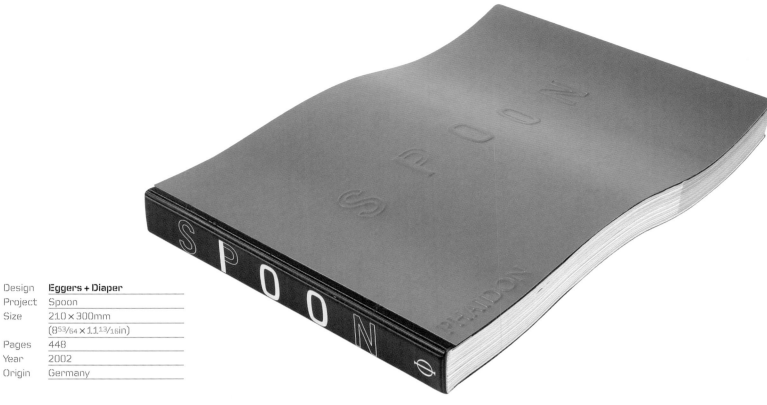

Design	**Eggers + Diaper**
Project	Spoon
Size	210 × 300mm
	(8⁵³/₆₄ × 11¹³/₁₆in)
Pages	448
Year	2002
Origin	Germany

The title of this book, featuring the work of 100 product designers, is reflected in its profile—a soft wave form similar to that of a spoon. The striking cover was created by stamping the title onto machine-bent sheets of metal. These sheets are bound to the endpapers of the book, causing the pages to gently follow the contours of the covers. Highly unusual, the pages of the book function very well, although storage can prove difficult as it cannot help but stand out in the bookcase.

Go to: A047   B008

Design	**2GD/2GraphicDesign**
Project	ToC.2GDIV
Size	200 × 100mm
	(7⅞ × 4in)
Pages	128
Year	2000
Origin	Denmark

Printed in black-and-magenta throughout, this small, dense manifesto for Danish design firm 2GD/2Graphic Design is printed entirely on tracing paper. Produced as a continuous concertina-folded document, the translucency of the paper allows the layers of information to build up and subside. The magenta is printed on one side of the paper and the black on the other; this gives the page a sense of depth that would not be possible were it printed on regular paper. The looseness of the binding allows the book to be opened out and interacted with.

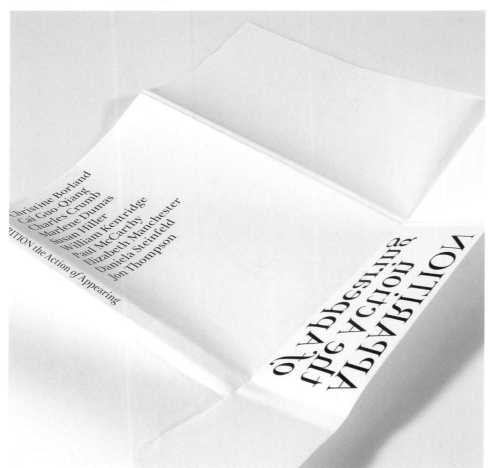

Design	**A2-GRAPHICS/SW/HK**
Project	Apparition: the Action of Appearing
Size	217 × 156mm (8 35/64 × 6 9/64in)
Pages	80
Year	2003
Origin	UK

Through the simple use of bible paper (40gsm uncoated) for the dust jacket of this art catalog, the designers achieved a clever twist. Printed in black only on one side of the sheet, the title of the exhibition is hidden, but is revealed, literally and conceptually, by folding the sheet back on itself. Because of the lightness of the paper used, a ghost of the type remains visible. Although very simple and frugal, the cover is striking and clever.

Go to: B030   B049 B058–B059

Design	**Carsten Nicolai/Olaf**
	Bender/Jonna Groendahl
Project	Auto Pilot: Carsten Nicolai
Size	230 × 170mm
	(9³/₆₄ × 6³/₄in)
Pages	104
Year	2002
Origin	Germany

The minimal lightness of this book is interrupted halfway through by a series of clear acetate sheets which have different sized and shaped black panels printed on them. As the plastic sheets are turned, the black-on-black image builds and changes. The build-up of pages makes for a beautifully dense and reflective field of black.

Go to: A047

Design	**Mode**
Project	Lostrobots
Size	290 × 230mm
	(11.1$^{13}/_{32}$ × 9$^3/_{64}$in)
Pages	Variable
Year	2003
Origin	UK

This portfolio was produced as a
limited-edition for a photographers'
agent. The special foiled surface of
the box seems to radiate heat and
light, as the color reacts to the light
source. The abstract logo is subtly
embossed on the surface.

Go to: B064–B065

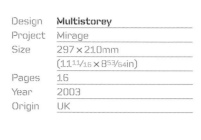

Design	**Multistorey**
Project	Mirage
Size	297 × 210mm
	(11.¹¹/16 × 8⁵³/64in)
Pages	16
Year	2003
Origin	UK

This brochure is constructed in reverse—a heavy card on the inside spread is covered in three layers of tracing paper, which are bound onto the front. To visually suggest the word mirage, an abstract image of the sun is printed on the inner card. The clothes were photographed back-lit on a model, creating near silhouettes, and printed on tracing paper. The translucency of the paper allows some of the image on the next page to show through, and the shapes formed by the model complement the adjacent shots. When bound together, the pages turn to give the illusion of the haze lifting, and of getting closer to the sun.

Design	**Raban Ruddigkeit**
Project	Freistil
Size	240 × 175mm
	(9⁷/₁₆ × 6⁵⁷/₆₄in)
Pages	476
Year	2003
Origin	Germany

This book showcases the best German commercial illustration. The cover boards are printed onto a special metallic mirrorboard which refracts light and color. The resulting spectrum is echoed on the spine.

Design	**Pentagram (J. Abbott Miller)**
Project	Scanning: The Aberrant Architectures of Diller + Scofidio
Size	292 × 207mm
	(11.1¹/₂ × 8⁹/₆₄in)
Pages	192
Year	2003
Origin	USA

The use of a lenticular image on the front of this book about the groundbreaking art/architectural practice Diller + Scofidio gives a taster of things to come. The cover image features a cocktail glass morphed with a hypodermic syringe. As the book is tilted, the syringe is injected into the base of the glass where it releases a lime-green liquid. The image is based on a design from the architects' series Vice/Virtue Glasses.

Go to: B019   B025   B053   B054   B055

Go to: B059

Design	**Sagmeister Inc.**
Project	Mariko Mori: Wave UFO
Size	290 × 236mm
	(11.13/32 × 9.19/64in)
Pages	174
Year	2003
Origin	USA

The cover of this book about the artist Mariko Mori uses a special light-reactive material. This creates a wide spectrum of colors as its surface refracts light. The constantly changing shimmer of color illustrates the artist's installations beautifully.

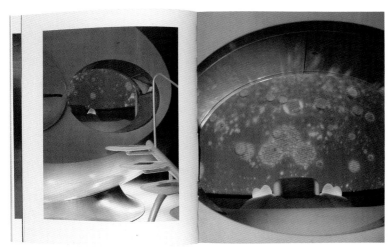

Go to: A050   A051   A056   B068   B074

Design   **Faydherbe/De Vringer**
Project   Dolly-Book
Size   246 × 176mm
           (9^{11}/$_{16}$ × 6^{15}/$_{16}$in)
Pages   32
Year   2001
Origin   The Netherlands

This type-specimen book was produced with two contrasting covers. Both use the same silver foil–blocked image of a bulldog. However, by using dark maroon flock, the cover is transformed into something very different. With its very tactile surface, flock can add a different language to a book.

Design   **COMA**
Project   The Smiths
Size   21.5 × 170mm
           (8^{15}/$_{32}$ × 6^{3}/$_{4}$in)
Pages   112
Year   2002
Origin   USA

This book shows the work of three artists: the renowned modernist Tony Smith and his two daughters, Kiki and Seton. The cover of the book uses fawn flock with the title debossed on its surface. A bellyband wrapped around the cover obscures this printing. Elements of all three artists are reflected in the cover; the typography is based on Tony's work, the size and scale of the book reflects Seton's work, and the cover material is inspired by Kiki's work. Thereby, all three personalities are united in this one simple cover.

Go to: B052

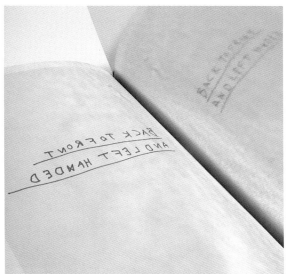

Design **Browns**
Project Blame Everyone Else
by Paul Davis
Size 332 × 248mm
(7⅞ × 4in)
Pages 148
Year 2003
Origin UK

The artworks by the illustrator Paul Davis are faithfully reproduced in this large monogram. The designers have used 14 different types of paper throughout the book to reflect the original material, which is often scribbled down on scraps of paper, or anything to hand. The stocks used include mirror paper, uncoated, a variety of colored papers, and cast-coated papers, among others.

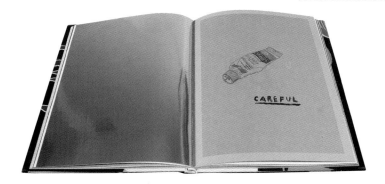

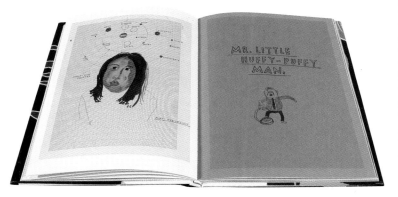

Design **Rose Design**
Project MFI, A Little Story:
Summer 2003
Size 296 × 210mm
(11.^{21}/$_{32}$ × 8^{53}/$_{64}$in)
Pages 16
Year 2003
Origin UK

This brochure was produced as an internal communication device for employees of the large British furniture store MFI. The brochure tells the story of an employee at a match factory who came up with the simple idea of sticking sandpaper to just one side of a box of matches instead of both. This simple idea saved the match company much time and money. The story is clearly illustrated through the box of matches shown on the front and back covers; on the front, a real strip of sandpaper is applied but on the back, there is none.

Go to: A043 B033 B066 B067 B071 B075

Experimental Formats.2

Books
Brochures
Catalogs

Roger Fawcett-Tang

Experimental Formats.2 13

Contents

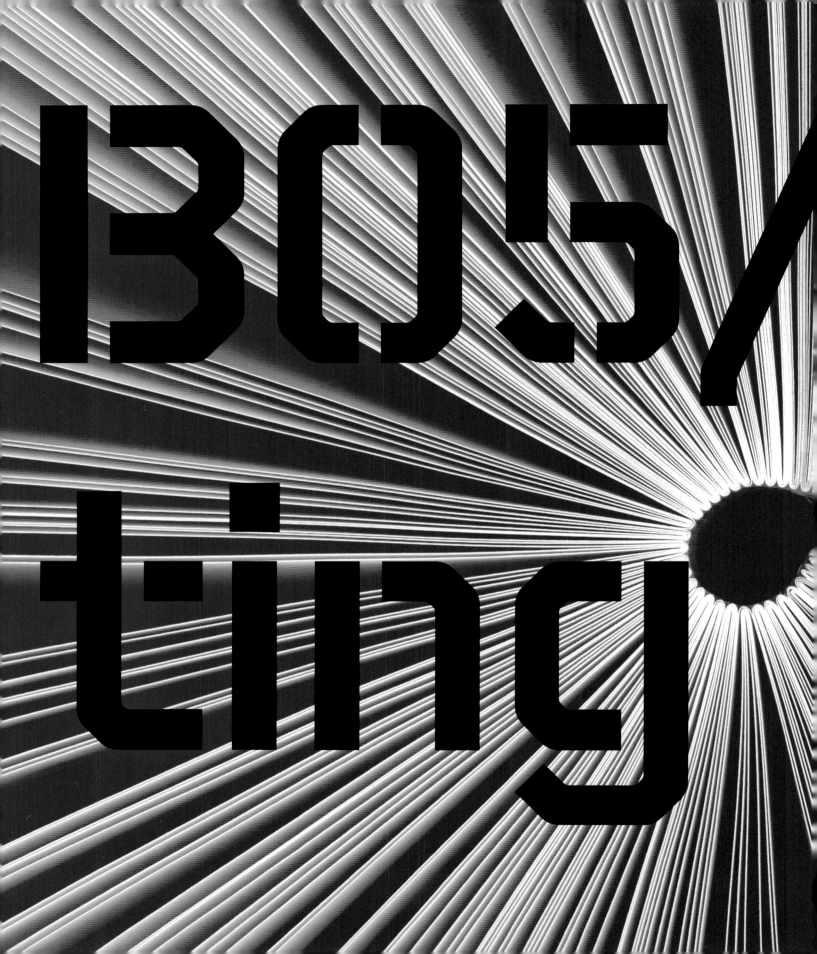

Prin

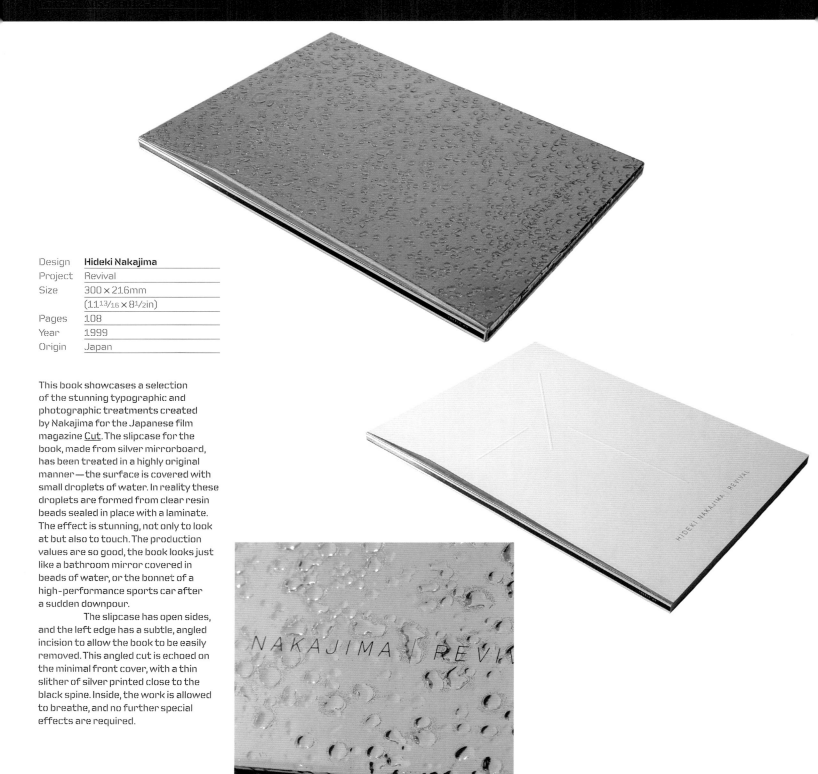

Design	**Hideki Nakajima**
Project	Revival
Size	300 × 216mm
	(11.$^{13}/_{16}$ × 8.$^1/_2$in)
Pages	108
Year	1999
Origin	Japan

This book showcases a selection of the stunning typographic and photographic treatments created by Nakajima for the Japanese film magazine <u>Cut</u>. The slipcase for the book, made from silver mirrorboard, has been treated in a highly original manner—the surface is covered with small droplets of water. In reality these droplets are formed from clear resin beads sealed in place with a laminate. The effect is stunning, not only to look at but also to touch. The production values are so good, the book looks just like a bathroom mirror covered in beads of water, or the bonnet of a high-performance sports car after a sudden downpour.

The slipcase has open sides, and the left edge has a subtle, angled incision to allow the book to be easily removed. This angled cut is echoed on the minimal front cover, with a thin slither of silver printed close to the black spine. Inside, the work is allowed to breathe, and no further special effects are required.

Design	**Intro**
Project	The Colour of White
Size	263 × 263mm
	(10^{23}/$_{64}$ × 10^{23}/$_{64}$in)
Pages	78
Year	2001
Origin	UK

This book, announcing the launch of an online art gallery, was sent out to an A-list group within the London art scene. To avoid any clash of egos, no images are shown on the cover or in the book. It is a pure blank canvas, which encourages the curious reader to refer to the Web site in order to gain a clearer understanding of the project.

The book is contained within a substantial, white, cloth-covered slipcase, with the title of the project embossed on the surface. The quality of production and delicacy of touch means this quiet book speaks volumes.

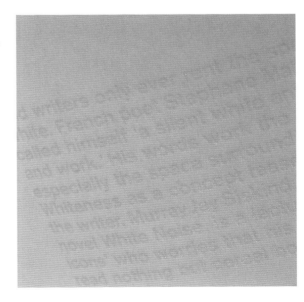

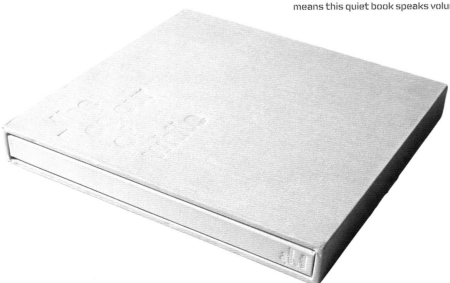

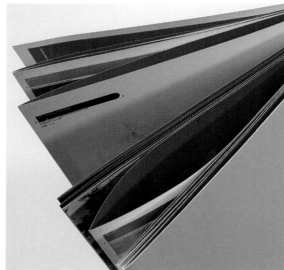

Design	**Eggers + Diaper**
Project	Susan Hiller: Recall
Size	266 × 225mm
	$(10^{15}/_{32} \times 8^{55}/_{64}\text{in})$
Pages	172
Year	2004
Origin	Germany

For this project, conceived as a conventional monograph for the artist Susan Hiller, the designer resolved an unrealized sound installation called Clinic, which was to feature dialog by a variety of people. This eight-page section subtly fades in from white to pale cream, deepening from the left side of the first page. The different transcriptions are set in a variety of typefaces and printed in a UV varnish.

Design	**Build**
Project	"TRVL" Visual Travelogue
Size	257 × 185mm
	(10.1/8 × 7.9/32in)
Pages	24
Year	2002
Origin	UK

This beautiful journal documents the
global travels of the designer through
a combination of photography and
diagrammatic means. French folded,
the inside folds are printed in
fluorescent pink, with diary entries and
supplementary information printed
white out. The full-color pages are
given another level of information
through the use of a gloss UV varnish
which holds further information.

The booklet was produced
as a supplement to issue 290 of the
Japanese design journal <u>Idea</u>.

Loch Assynt
Morar Sands
Moray Firth
Skye
North Uist

Home
Work
Social
Visit
Listen

1999–2003

Design	**Hector Pottie**
Project	Home Work Social Visit
	Listen 1999–2003
Size	250 × 187mm
	(9²⁷/₃₂ × 7³/₈in)
Pages	60
Year	2004
Origin	UK

Produced to accompany an exhibition
in Berlin that featured a series of silk-
screened Ordinance Survey (the UK's
national mapping agency) maps,
focusing on the areas in which the
designer grew up. The maps were
produced as solid colors to draw
attention to the beautiful coastlines
and lakes.

The book uses the same silk-
screened maps, but here they are
overprinted to create rich, abstract
patterns. These abstracted maps are
complemented by another mapping
process, with which the designer
charted his location and interests
over the past five years. The pagination
of the book is seemingly random, with
a variety of cover designs appearing
on different copies.

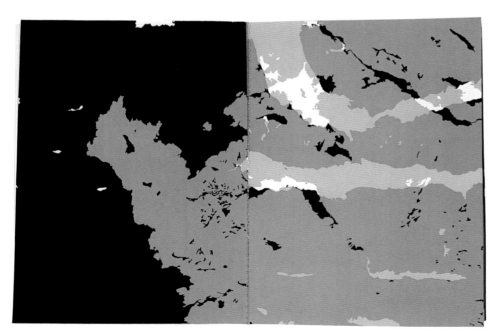

Design **Irma Boom**
Project Light Years:
         Zumtobel 2000 1.950
Size   223 × 1.92mm
         (8^{25}/$_{32}$ × 7^{35}/$_{64}$in)
Pages   624
Year   2000
Origin   The Netherlands

Produced to celebrate the fiftieth
anniversary of this large lighting
company, standard chronological order
is reversed in this book. It starts with
the present day and, as the pages are
flipped, the clock is turned back until,
by the end of the book the reader is
in 1950, at the birth of the company.
The cover features a series of colored
circles acting as a set of spotlights
trained on its cover. However, combined,
these lights form a black center, not
a bright light. This dense mass is
enlivened by a gloss UV-varnished
spiral which glints in the light.

          The spine, the only place the
title appears, is printed in luminescent
ink that glows in a dark environment.
The fore-edge features a series of
50 color-coded lines that are used
to indicate the year.

Design	**Hideki Nakajima**
Project	Ryuichi Sakamoto: Sampled Life
Size	308 × 230mm
	(12¹⁄₈ × 9³⁄₆₄in)
Pages	195 + various booklets
Year	1999
Origin	Japan

This package was produced to accompany Japanese composer Ryuichi Sakamoto's opera Life. It is comprised of four books; Score and Interview, Diary, Pictures, and Text, plus various loose-leaf elements, all housed within a special cardboard box.

Of the books, Text is the most lavish, though it continues the same monochromatic minimal theme as the rest of the package. The high-gloss white cover has the title printed in an off-white varnish and three vertical rules embossed on the surface; these rules are embossed in the same position on every internal page as well. The spine of the book is printed with a luminescent ink that radiates a green light in the darkness.

Inside, the discrete English, German, and Japanese typographies flow across the pages, with key words highlighted in a UV varnish. Other texts have been rendered illegible by printing a black rule over the words, allowing just a fragment of the top and bottom of each character to remain visible. A white line has been used in the same way, leaving the vaguest trace of letterforms behind.

The second part of the book features a series of foldout pages printed with images of the composer's studio and working environment. These foldouts are not immediately accessible: the pages have been sprayed with a light adhesive which compels the reader to force the pages open to reveal what is inside.

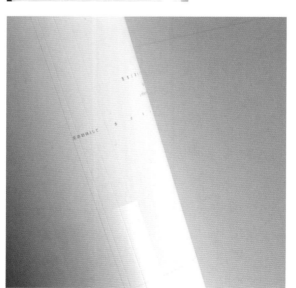

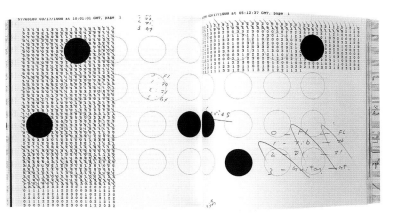

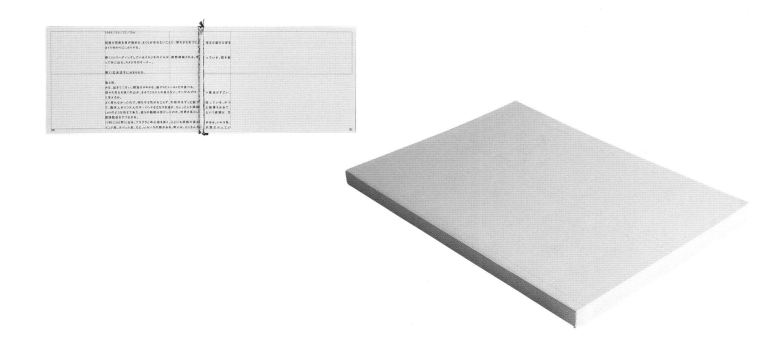

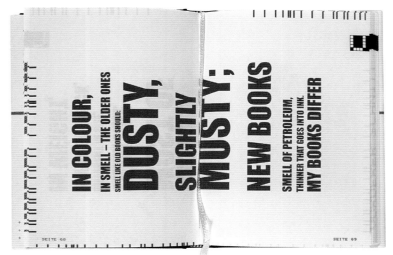

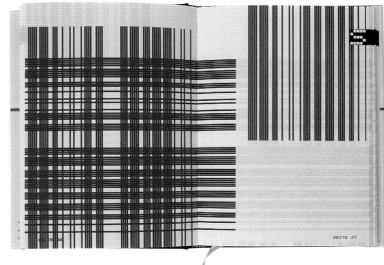

Design	Robert Schäfer
Project	Das Buchobjekt
Size	249 × 148 × 70mm
	($9^{13}/_{16}$ × $5^3/_{16}$ × $2^{49}/_{64}$in)
Pages	194
Year	1999
Origin	Germany

This elaborately packaged design book
makes full use of fore-edge printing.
Although printed in only two colors—
red and black—the book remains
exciting and visually fresh on every
spread. The edge printing, which only
becomes fully readable if the pages are
fanned slightly, breaks away from the
edge of the book at times to extend
across the page, producing abstract
bar codes or gingham patterns.

Design	**Michael Nash Associates**
	+ Jane
Project	Blue
Size	265 × 210mm
	(10$^{7/16}$ × 8$^{53/64}$in)
Pages	48
Year	2000
Origin	UK

This catalog was produced to accompany a group exhibition at the Walsall Gallery in Birmingham, England. The upper right corner of the cover has been removed, to echo the gallery's logo. The title has been die cut from the fluorescent orange cover to reveal fragments of the names of artists involved in the show. As the overall theme of the show was the color blue, the use of orange makes for a jarring mental contrast. It also plays a visual trick on the retina; as the reader focuses on the title page, the white paper appears blue as their eyes overcompensate for the vibrant orange. The gatefolded back cover includes the same die-cut lettering.

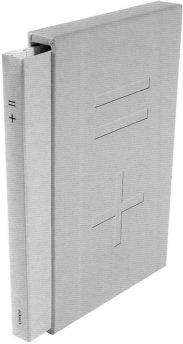

Design	**Ph.D**
Project	Dickson's: The Science of Sensation
Size	225 × 164mm
	(8⁵⁶/₆₄ × 6²⁹/₆₄in)
Pages	16
Year	2004
Origin	USA

Produced for Dickson's, a specialist printers, this brochure utilizes every unusual printing process in the company's vast arsenal. Contained within a color coordinated slipcase, the wiro-bound brochure protrudes, revealing a cloth-effect spine. Inside, each "page" is a pocket containing an additional sheet of paper. The pages feature embossing and debossing, letterpress printing, foil blocking, thermography ...

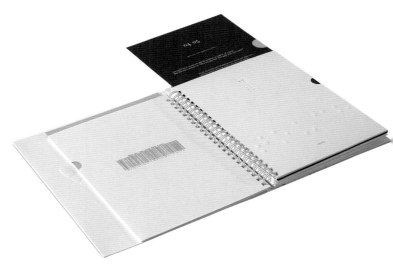

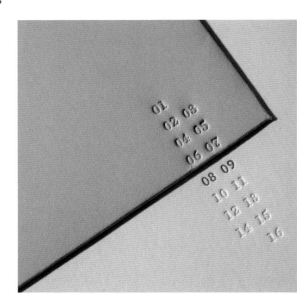

Design	**SEA Design**
Project	Wim Crouwel: Seen/Unseen
Size	264 × 209mm
	(10^{25}/$_{64}$ × 8^{1}/$_{4}$in)
Pages	32
Year	2003
Origin	UK

Produced to accompany an exhibition of the work of the living legend Wim Crouwel, this catalog reflects the vibrant style of the Dutchman, while retaining characteristic elements of SEA Design. The cover uses the Crouwel font Soft Alphabet, originally designed for a Claus Oldenberg poster. The keyline version of the type printed in orange is precisely embossed, giving the cover another dimension. This subtle embossing is more visible on the inside front cover, where it is printed in a solid copper.

The main section of the catalog features French-folded pages on uncoated stock. At the back of the book, a series of Crouwel's font designs are reproduced, printed on a light bible paper.

Sauna is the most widely used Finnish word. In 142 languages it has the same form – except in Swedish. Not a coincidence, of course. Our word is *bastu*. But yes, Swedish *bastu* is not a real sauna, anyway.

¶ INGRID HOLSTEIN (29), an interior designer in Lund, Sweden

[16]

Keep this door closed

TEXT GETS READABLE IN SAUNA [> 80 DEGREES CELSIUS]

[17]

Henrik Birkvig

DESIGNERS' SECRET SAUNA STORIES

Sauna is the most widely used Finnish word. In 142 languages it has the same form – except in Swedish. Not a coincidence, of course. Our word is *bastu*. But yes, Swedish *bastu* is not a real sauna, anyway.

¶ INGRID HOLSTEIN (29), an interior designer in Lund, Sweden

Keep this door closed

TEXT GETS READABLE IN SAUNA [> 80 DEGREES CELSIUS]

[16]   [17]

Kurt Weidemann

DESIGNERS' SECRET SAUNA STORIES   TEXT GETS READABLE IN SAUNA [> 80 DEGREES CELSIUS]

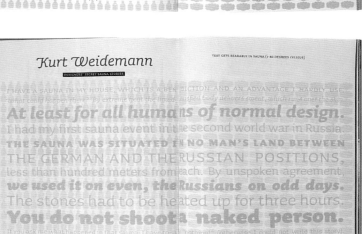

Kurt Weidemann

DESIGNERS' SECRET SAUNA STORIES   TEXT GETS READABLE IN SAUNA [> 80 DEGREES CELSIUS]

I HAVE A SAUNA IN MY HOUSE, WHICH IS A BENEDICTION AND AN ADVANTAGE. I HARDLY USE what could happen to the extreme heat the finest naked body delivers sweat, which runs over the skin.
At least for all humans of normal design.
I had my first sauna event in the second world war in Russia.
THE SAUNA WAS SITUATED IN NO MAN'S LAND BETWEEN THE GERMAN AND THE RUSSIAN POSITIONS, less than hundred meters from each. By unspoken agreement, **we used it on even, the Russians on odd days.** The stones had to be heated up for three hours. **You do not shoot a naked person.**
If you ask me what happened in that sauna, I have to say "nothing!" (otherwise I could not write this story).

Design	**Underware/Piet Schreuders**
Project	Read Naked
Size	205 × 184mm
	(8³/₃₂ × 7¹/₄in)
Pages	48
Year	2002
Origin	The Netherlands

This type-specimen book goes beyond the realms of the standard four-page leaflet often sent out to announce a new font design. The name of the font—Sauna—is the starting point for this elaborate production.

Printed on a special stock that is capable of withstanding temperatures of up to 248°F (120°C), the paper has a unique tactile quality. Some pages are even printed with a humidity-controlled ink that only becomes visible inside a sauna, where it reveals hidden messages, although design studios tend not to have sauna facilities in-house!

Design	**Pentagram (Paula Scher)**
Project	Make it Bigger
Size	165 × 235mm
	(6½ × 9¼in)
Pages	272
Year	2002
Origin	USA

Visually illustrating the title of this designer's monograph, the large scale typography extends beyond the limits of the book's format. The type is printed off the front cover and onto the edges of the book. The effect is to produce a solid black-and-orange typographic block.

Go to: B021

Design	**3 Deep Design**
Project	Amplification. Jeff Busby
Size	31.8 × 21.5mm
	(12½ × 8½in)
Pages	48
Year	2002
Origin	Australia

The incredibly high luster of this photography book contradicts the auto carnage of the images. The beautiful photography of Jeff Busby is allowed to speak for itself, printed full bleed, spread after spread. The entire book is overprinted with a high gloss UV varnish which not only brings further richness to the images, but also makes the pages adhere to each other. This adhesion prevents the pages from being casually flicked — each page has to be peeled open to reveal its treasures.

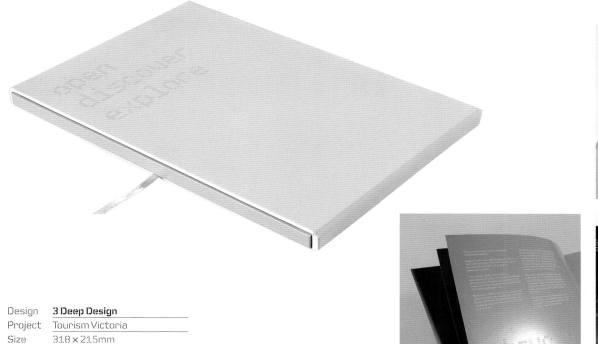

Design	**3 Deep Design**
Project	Tourism Victoria
Size	318 × 215mm
	(12½ × 8½in)
Pages	64
Year	2004
Origin	Australia

Housed in an elegant white slipcase, this lavish brochure was produced for a tourism conference in Melbourne, Australia. The headline typeface used throughout the brochure was specifically designed for the project; the grid used for the letterforms is based on the street plan of the city's Central Business District.

The images are all printed as tritone black and whites, which gives them great depth. The cover and slipcase feature the grid font foil-blocked in a clear varnish and silver.

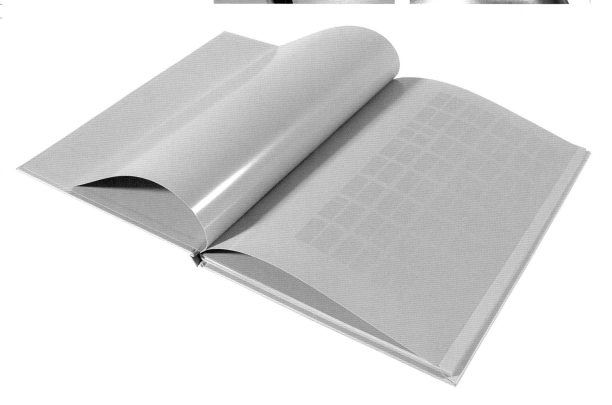

Design	**Made Thought**
Project	Bill Brandt catalog
Size	224 × 165mm
	(8¹³/₁₆ × 6³¹/₆₄in)
Pages	32
Year	2003
Origin	UK

The catalog produced for Focus Gallery's inaugural exhibition, <u>Bill Brandt</u>, was made available with three different belly bands, each featuring a cropped fragment from one of the photographer's images. This otherwise conventional saddle-stitched catalog incorporates an extended cover section that wraps back around itself to form eight internal panels onto which small reproductions of Brandt's images appear.

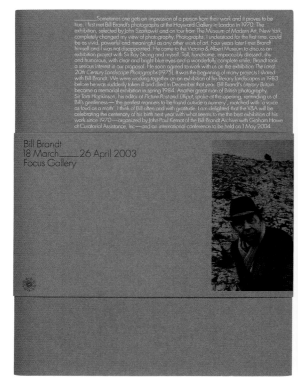

Go to: A076   B019   B053   B054   B055

Design	**Pentagram (J. Abbott Miller)**
Project	Scanning: The Aberrant Architectures of Diller + Scofidio
Size	292 × 207mm
	(11.1½ × 8⁹/₆₄in)
Pages	192
Year	2003
Origin	USA

This book about the groundbreaking art/architectural practice Diller + Scofidio features French-folded pages throughout. However, the folds are perforated, tempting the reader to tear the pages open to reveal their hidden secrets. At the center of the folded edge a curve has been cut out, increasing the temptation to pull the pages apart.

The external pages feature text and the work of the architectural practice, while the internal pages show video stills of banal office interiors, shot as if taken from CCTV footage.

Design	**Project M Team**
Project	Project M
Size	228 × 150mm
	(8⁹/₁₆ × 5²⁹/₃₂in)
Pages	260
Year	2004
Origin	USA

This simple, red-covered book features black-and-white images of all the designers involved in the project together with images of their working environment. These drab, monochrome images are broken up by a series of thin fragments of type printed white out of the images at a 45° angle. In this state, the book offers little of visual interest, however, with a little time and effort the book's hidden message can be revealed. By folding the top corner of each page into the spine, the white fragments of type start to form recognizable letters. As the type reads from both left to right and right to left, the statement is not readable until the final pages are folded revealing "think wrong."

In this form, the book becomes a 3-D object that refuses to be closed.

Go to: A039   A040   Go to: A054

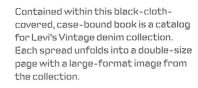

Design	**The Kitchen**
Project	"No"
Size	218 × 244mm
	(8¹⁹/₃₂ × 9³⁹/₆₄in)
Pages	72
Year	2002
Origin	UK

Contained within this black-cloth-covered, case-bound book is a catalog for Levi's Vintage denim collection. Each spread unfolds into a double-size page with a large-format image from the collection.

Design	**Fabrica**
Project	2398 gr.: A Book About Food
Size	280 × 222mm
	(11 × 8¾in)
Pages	320
Year	2003
Origin	Italy

This elaborate book about food from the Italian design collective Fabrica tempts the reader into its pages. The book features sections printed on a white, coated stock and a cream, uncoated stock. Two of the cream sections feature French folds; the first is simply folded, with full-color images reproduced on the hidden insides, offering only a glimpse to the reader. In the second section the folds are perforated, which allows the reader to tear open the pages to reveal their hidden content fully.

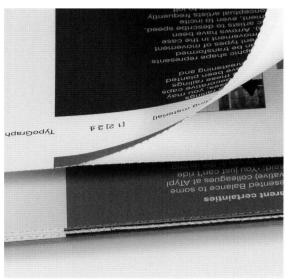

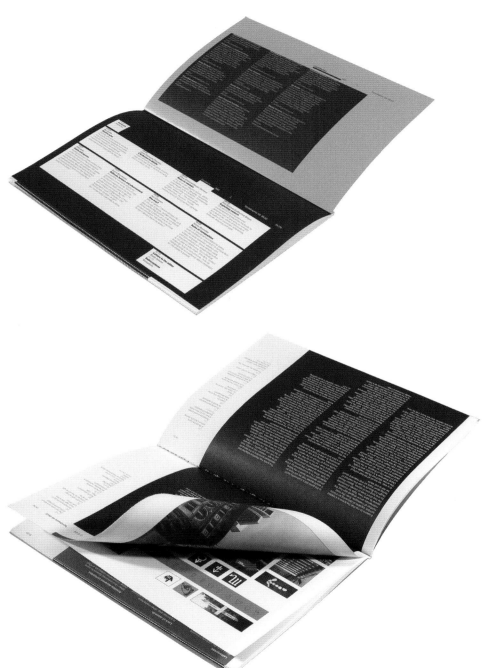

Design	**Sans + Baum**
Project	ISTD TypoGraphic 59 "Back to Type"
Size	297 × 213mm (11.43/64 × 8.25/64in)
Pages	40
Year	2004
Origin	UK

This edition of the everchanging type journal features a clever series of folded pages, printed in two and four colors that are combined to get the most from special colors and four-color reproductions.

The elaborate pagination of the journal works in such a way as to switch between perforated French folds and standard single pages. The outside of each page is purely typographic, and printed in a range of special colors. Once the perforated French folds have been torn open, images for each of the essays are revealed. Most of the image sections are printed in two special colors, with four-color spreads used where necessary.

Design A2-GRAPHICS/SW/HK

Project	Recognition
Size	210 x 158mm
	(8⁵³⁄₆₄ x 6¹⁵⁄₆₄mm)
Pages	128
Year	2003
Origin	UK

One venue and one catalog, but two dust jackets, two curators, two shows, and four artists. The multiple content of this catalog is realized through the two dust jackets protecting the cover. Each jacket is folded horizontally so that when the two are wrapped around the book, the group title becomes legible.

 The jackets were also used as invites to the private viewing, with the details hidden on the inside of the folded sheet. Each show was assigned a particular color: green for the first and red for the second. These colors are used inside the book (to highlight key pieces of text relating to the relevant show) and on the reverse of the relevant jackets.

Design	**Purtill Family Business**
Project	Tuttle: In Parts, 1998–2001
Size	241 x 166mm
	(9³¹/₆₄ x 6¹⁷/₃₂in)
Pages	52
Year	2001
Origin	United States

This book reproduces, at actual size, a series of paintings titled <u>Painted Boxes,</u> by the artist Richard Tuttle. Each painting is reproduced on a large sheet of paper that is folded down and bound into the book.

    The book is bound with a rubberized glue similar to that used on jotter pads. This gives the sections great flexibility and allows the option of pulling the sections apart without causing damage.

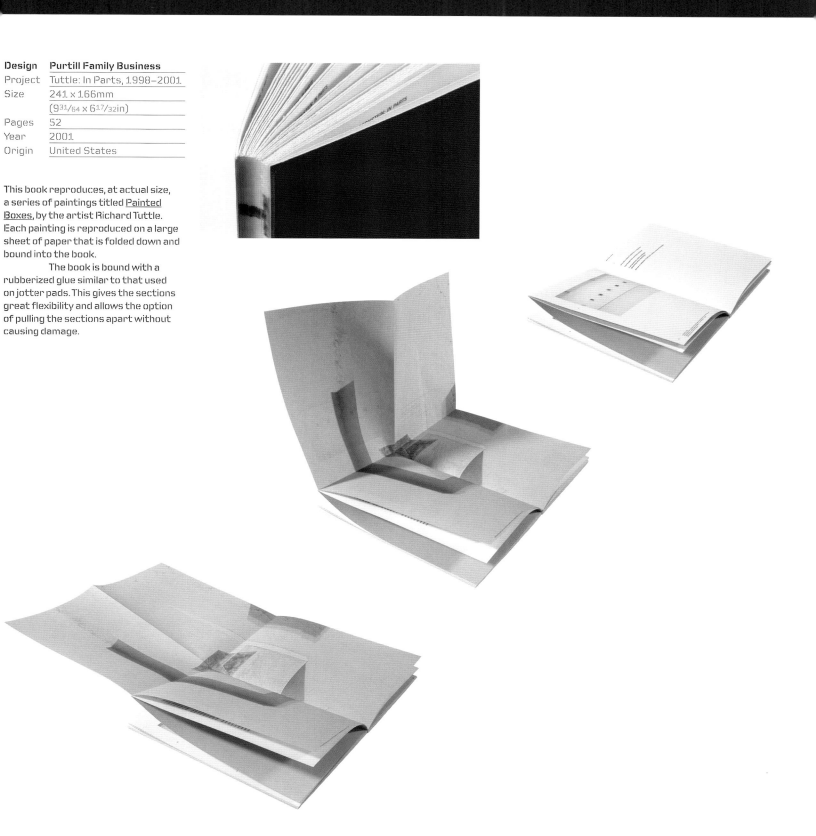

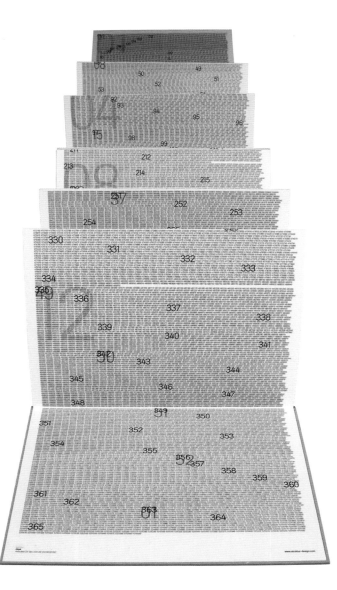

Design	**Struktur Design**
Project	Minutes
Size	223 × 164mm
	(8²⁵/₃₂ × 6²⁹/₆₄in)
Pages	36
Year	2002
Origin	UK

This self-promotional diary explores the rhythmic typographic patterns generated by sequential numbers. Printed in fluorescent pink, the 365 days of the year are broken down into 10-minute intervals, starting at one, and running consecutively through to 525,600. This series of numbers is overprinted in warm gray and black to indicate the days, weeks, and months of the year.

The continuous flow of typographic information is concertina-folded into the front and back covers. The back of the diary works as a more conventional "book," with the days of the year broken into the 12 months. When unfolded, the diary extends to nearly 10ft (3m) in length.

Design	**Rose Design**
Project	Westzone Publishing: Preview, Spring 2001
Size	210 × 148mm ($8^{53}/_{64}$ × $5^{13}/_{16}$in)
Pages	38
Year	2001
Origin	UK

This edition of Westzone Publishing's catalog features a series of perforated, French-folded pages and die-cut panels.

Each spread showcases a different book from the publisher's list, with text on the right-hand page, and the title and a rectangular, die-cut hole in the center of the left page. The hole reveals a fragment of an image, a cropped-in detail, a taster. This encourages the reader to tear open the French-folded pages in order to reveal the full image.

Design	**Base Design**
Project	Serge Leblon
Size	255 × 212mm
	$(10^{1}/_{32} \times 8^{11}/_{32}\text{in})$
Pages	68
Year	2000
Origin	Belgium/Spain/USA

When within its minimal white slipcase, all attention is directed to the raw spine of this book. No text appears on the slipcase, just a sequence of dots, one for each letter of the photographer's name, Serge Leblon. With the slipcase removed, the rationale for the unusual spine is revealed—the book has been ripped open at the central spread and folded back on itself. Upon closer inspection this destructive act is not what it seems; it has been bound this way deliberately. Halfway through the book lies the now redundant cover, which is case-bound in white cloth with the photographer's name embossed in a dot matrix font, echoing the series of dots on the slipcase.

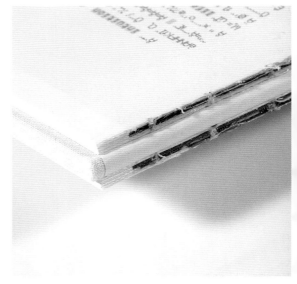

Design	**FL@33**
Project	Coup de Grace/
	Zwischenstation
Size	225 × 155mm
	(8⁵⁵/₆₄ × 6⁷/₆₄in)
Pages	60 loose sheets
Year	1997
Origin	Germany

The work of two very different poets is housed within this special double-fronted cover/folder. Their distinct styles are clearly illustrated; the expressive energy of Bartosz Maj's Zwischenstation cover is in complete contrast to the understated simplicity of Gernot Heinkelein's Coup de Grace front. These two very different typographic styles are continued throughout the loose-leaf pages of their respective books.

Produced as a strictly limited edition of just 100 copies, the book has a strong craft feel to it. The cover is embossed and printed in white letterpress ink, and the loose sheets are held in order with a simple bellyband. The decision not to bind the pages allows readers the freedom to explore the books in any order, and removes any linear narrative from the different poems.

Design	**Made Thought**
Project	Thinking Big: Concepts for
	Twenty-First Century
	British Sculpture
Size	215 × 154mm
	(8^15/32 × 6^4/64in)
Pages	48 + 176
Year	2002
Origin	UK

Two traditionally bound books have been cleverly joined, back-to-back, to present two perspectives of a sculpture exhibition. The book comes inside a gray, typographic, open-ended slipcase to keep the two volumes from unfolding.

The smaller, 48-page volume contains essays on and information about each of the featured artists. The larger volume showcases beautiful photographic details of each of the sculptures, focusing in on small details and textures.

The Z-shaped, double-spined cover allows the two volumes to work both independently and together.

Design	**Sans + Baum**
Project	In Sight: A Guide to Design with Low Vision in Mind
Size	216 × 152mm
	(8¹/₂ × 5³¹/₃₂in)
Pages	2 × 152
Year	2004
Origin	UK

Housed within a conventional hardback cover, this guide to design legibility for the visually impaired opens up to reveal two separate books. The book on the left contains all the text set at a legibly large point size. The book on the right contains all visual material related to the text section with reference numbers linking the two separate sections together.

Using such a large point size for the text made it impossible to integrate the text and image properly, hence the designers used this system of two parallel volumes. The binding system was well received when shown to a group of people with varying types of visual impairment.

Design	Bohatsch Graphic Design
Project	Delugan_Meissl 2
Size	227 × 164mm
	(8^{15}/$_{16}$ × 6^{29}/$_{64}$in)
Pages	156 + 184
Year	2001
Origin	Austria

The binding system for this book about
an Austrian architectural practice
neatly links two separate case-bound
books. One volume covers concepts
while the other documents realized
buildings; the clever binding enables the
reader to cross-reference the two
with regard to particular projects.

The double-hinged cover
provides great flexibility, allowing
each book to be read independently
of the other, but also enabling certain
spreads in the different volumes to
work together, and images to bleed
from one volume to the other. The
books are housed in an open-ended
slipcase, sealed with a yellow tracing-
paper bellyband.

Die rückseitige, demontagewandte Fassade des so genannten Baikens in der Boxer Denia-City erzeugt die Bild einer Verkehrsmaschine und der Verkehr, die Erschließung ist auch ein zentrales Element des Entwurfes. Die gewaltige Dimension des Gebäudes wird nicht nur durch seine Kubatur, sondern auch durch die Darstellung der Wege, die zum Funktionieren nötig sind.

Facing away from the main Danube, the rear façade of the so-called Beam in eastern Danau-City creates the image of a traffic machine; traffic, circulation and access are indeed the central elements of the design. The massive scale of the building is communicated not only through its cubature, its volume, but also through the resolution of the paths necessary for its function(s).

Dramatisiert und inszeniert die unterschiedlichen Erschließungswege zu den Wohnungen. Verglaste Laubengänge, skulptural ausgebildete Freitreppen, punktuell eingeordnete Liftgruppen. Thema die Veröffentlichung des Weges zur eigenen Wohnung.

Dramatising and dramatically staged the various access routes to the apartments. Glazed, enclosed walkways, sculptural external staircases, individually grouped elevators. The theme: publicising the path to ones own apartment.

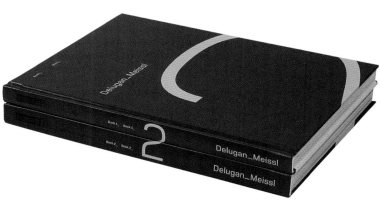

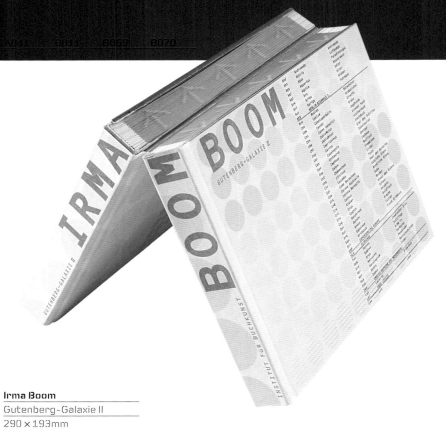

Design	**Irma Boom**
Project	Gutenberg-Galaxie II
Size	290 × 193mm
	(11^{13}/$_{32}$ × 7^{19}/$_{32}$in)
Pages	2 × 208
Year	2002
Origin	The Netherlands

This limited-edition monograph on and by the Dutch designer Irma Boom comes wrapped in a printed sheet of brown paper. This gives the impression that the book is large and portrait format. However, when the wrapping paper is removed, the book folds in half to form two smaller, landscape books of 145 × 193mm (5^{45}/$_{64}$ × 7^{19}/$_{32}$in). The top book illustrates details such as the intricate binding and printing methods used for books that Boom has designed, and the lower book displays full spreads and covers from them.

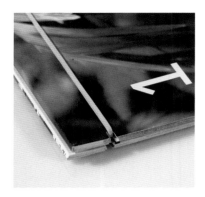

Design	**Base Design**
Project	Women'secret Look Book: Spring/Summer 2003
Size	205 × 143mm (8⁵/₆₄ × 5⁵/₈in)
Pages	24 + 16
Year	2003
Origin	Spain/Belgium/USA

This fashion book is broken into two separate booklets, both keeping to the same size and format. The loose pages are held together simply with a rubber band. This is kept in position by a notch that has been cut out of the top and bottom of each page. This binding method allows the pages a good degree of flexibility and movement as they are turned.

Design	**Blast**
Project	Workout 2004
Size	105 × 148mm
	(4⁹/₆₄ × 5⁵³/₆₄in)
Pages	16 + 72
Year	2003
Origin	UK

This small pocket booklet for the British D&AD features information about a series of courses and seminars on creativity. The first section is a standard saddle-stitched booklet, bound into the outer cover. The second section features loose-leaf pages that have been bound into the outer cover with a thick rubber band. The band is kept in place by the notch cut into the top and bottom of each page and of the cover.

A bellyband wraps around the whole booklet, and as a pun on the title, the band has a measuring tape design printed on it.

Design	**Projekttriangle**
Project	Form+Farbe
Size	99 × 210mm
	(3⁷⁄₈ × 8⁵³⁄₆₄in)
Pages	26
Year	2000
Origin	Germany

The binding of this artist's brochure has been stripped back to the simplest method possible. The series of loose pages are sandwiched between two sheets of thick, gray board and held together by a thick red rubber band. Color is kept to a minimum, with the exception of one red page and a sheet of translucent yellow tracing paper that is laid over the word 'Farbe' (color). No page numbers appear in the brochure, which encourages the reader to interact and shuffle the pages into different sequences.

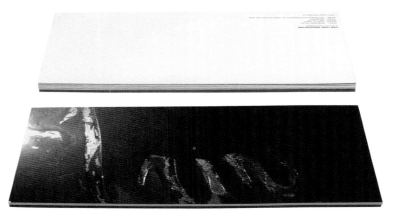

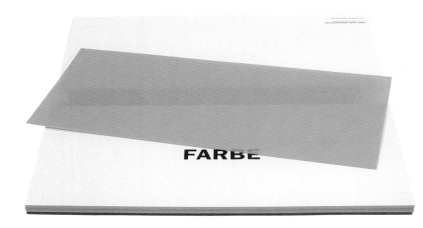

Design	**Cartlidge Levene**
Project	9 Kean Street, Covent Garden
Size	248 × 170mm (9⁴⁹/₆₄ × 6³/₄in)
Pages	44 + 32
Year	2001
Origin	UK

Produced to promote a series of luxury flat conversions in an old warehouse building in Covent Garden, London, this lavish property brochure incorporates two books. The first, printed on a gloss-coated stock, features a series of images of the building and its surroundings, mainly shot at night. The second, printed on an uncoated stock, mainly in black-and-white or warm gray, gives technical specifications and floor plans, together with images of the building in its unrenovated state.

The two volumes are bound into one double-spined W cover, the central fold of which is perforated, allowing them to also be pulled apart and used as conventional books.

Design	**Spin**
Project	Droogdokkenpark: Project²
Size	301 × 305mm
	(11.^{27}/$_{32}$ × 12in)
Pages	24 + 34
Year	2002
Origin	UK

This document on the proposed redevelopment of a dockland/warehouse area in Antwerp, Belgium, is presented within a large, square slipcase. The brochure is split into two separate volumes. Book 1, printed on an uncoated stock, features a series of images of the building in its present condition, together with the credentials of the three shortlisted architectural practices. Book 2, printed on a gloss-coated stock, features the architect's proposed concepts for the redevelopment.

      Both the books have minimal, dark gray, loose dust jackets. Removing these reveals their elegant Singer-sewn binding.

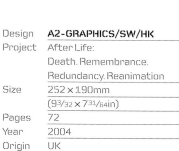

Design	**Eg.G**
Project	Quarantine
Size	198 × 150mm
	(7^{25}/$_{32}$ × 5^{29}/$_{32}$in)
Pages	20
Year	2003
Origin	UK

Produced for a theater production company, this small booklet features the group's projects, ideas, and research. The six-page cover wraps around from the inside back, where it is bound to the main body of the book with two nickel-plated binding screws.

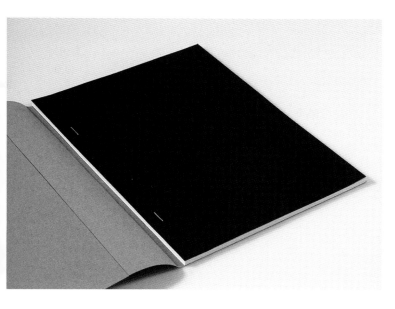

Design	**A2-GRAPHICS/SW/HK**
Project	After Life: Death. Remembrance. Redundancy. Reanimation
Size	252 × 190mm
	(9^{3}/$_{32}$ × 7^{31}/$_{64}$in)
Pages	72
Year	2004
Origin	UK

Resembling a dusty old school textbook from the 1970s, this cover belies the contemporary art contained within. The dust jacket is printed letterpress onto a cheap pulp stock, and with this removed, the simple binding method is revealed. The loose sheets of the book have been stapled through from front to back—another old-fashioned binding technique that increases the sense of nostalgia.

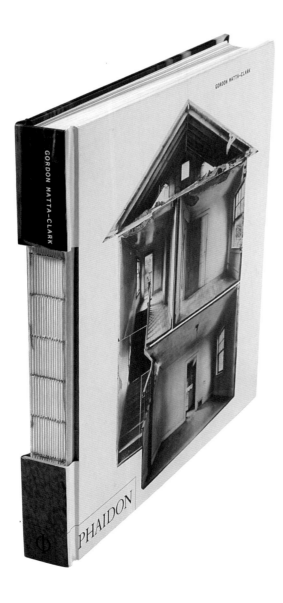

Design	**Julia Hasting**
Project	Gordon Matta-Clark
Size	257 × 256mm
	(10 1/8 × 10 5/64 in)
Pages	238
Year	2003
Origin	UK

This monograph on the American artist utilizes the same esthetic as that the artist is most famous for.

Matta-Clark's most notorious activity involved the dissection of disused buildings, either commercial or residential. He would slice through the structure to reveal the hidden internal construction. The design of the book has taken this practice to heart; a section has been cut out of the book's case-bound spine to reveal its construction. By using a vibrantly colored thread for the sewn sections, the spine has greater beauty. The colored thread, which appears on the central spread of each of the sections, adds color and brings attention to the book's construction.

Go to : A064 B036 B044 Go to : B049

Design	**Base Design**
Project	Amat Finques
Size	300 × 230mm
	(11.11³/₁₆ × 9³/₆₄in)
Pages	16
Year	2000
Origin	Spain/Belgium/USA

This modest brochure, produced for a long-established, Spanish property company, avoids the conventional binding method of saddle stitching. The 16 pages have been sewn through with red thread to match the color of the typography. The cover has a 2mm (¹/₄in), crease-folded spine, down the center of which the red thread runs.

Design	**Eg.G**
Project	Onitsuka Tiger
Size	150 × 160mm
	(5²⁹/₃₂ × 6¹⁹/₆₄in)
Pages	2 × 14
Year	2004
Origin	UK

Contained within a purpose-made box, the two thin editions of this sports shoe brochure are given precious quality. Both collections are bound in the traditional Japanese manner, with red thread. The attention to detail adds value and a sense of delicacy to the brochures.

Design	**COMA**
Project	Glee: Painting Now
Size	166 × 124mm
	(6^{17}/$_{32}$ × 4^{3}/$_{4}$in)
Pages	66 + 40
Year	2000
Origin	USA

This small, cloth-covered, case-bound book, produced to coincide with a group show of contemporary artists, looks quite conventional from the outside. However, once opened, the two sections are revealed.

Bound to the inside left cover is a book containing a series of images of the artists' work. The book is bound with a soft glue, allowing individual pages to be removed easily and used as postcards. The book on the right features essays and information about the artists.

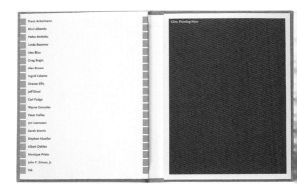

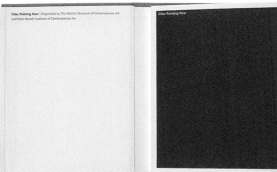

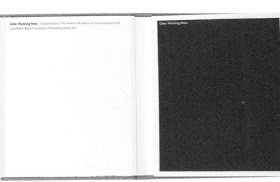

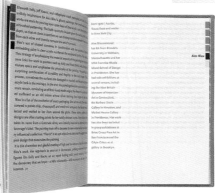

Design	**Pentagram (J. Abbott Miller)**
Project	Matthew Barney:
	The Cremaster Cycle
Size	322 × 235mm
	(12^{11}/$_{16}$ × 9^{1}/$_4$in)
Pages	528
Year	2002
Origin	USA

This vast, weighty book features the
complex work of artist Matthew
Barney. The book's title is printed on
the soft, clear PVC dust jacket, which
reveals the iconography and symbolism
of The Cremaster Cycle, foil blocked in
silver on the cloth cover beneath.
      The five parts of the cycle
are each given a curved index indent on
the fore-edge of the book.

Design	**Aufuldish & Warinner**
Project	The Logan Collection:
	A Portrait of our Times
	A Collector's Odyssey
	and Philosophy
Size	292 × 21.4mm
	(11.1^{1}/$_2$ × 8^{27}/$_{64}$in)
Pages	224
Year	2002
Origin	USA

This book showcases a private
collection of contemporary art.
Each chapter opens with a vibrant,
fluorescent green page. Thumb tabs
of the same color appear on the fore-
edge. These tabs allow the green to
appear on every spread, and always
reveal the previous two tabs on the
left edge and the following two tabs
on the right edge.

Design	**Pentagram (J. Abbott Miller)**
Project	Whitney Biennial 2000
Size	255 × 202mm
	(10^1/$_{32}$ × 7^{31}/$_{32}$in)
Pages	272
Year	2000
Origin	USA

The problem of how to present a large and varied selection of contemporary artists together without inviting comparisons is cleverly resolved in this publication. Produced to coincide with the Whitney Biennial exhibition in 2000, at the Whitney Museum of American Art in New York, the book alternates between two different stocks, from page to page. Images appear on coated pages without folios, and a yellow, uncoated stock is used for dividing pages, which hold the artist's name and information, together with picture captions. These yellow pages have been trimmed 1in (25mm) shorter than the image pages to permit a glimpse of the following artist's work, while not interfering with the work being viewed.

Go to: A076 B019 B025 B053 B054

Go to: A060–A061 B032

Design **Pentagram (J. Abbott Miller)**
Project Whitney Biennial 2002
Size 255 × 205mm
 (10^{1}/$_{32}$ × 8^{3}/$_{32}$in)
Pages 292
Year 2002
Origin USA

Featuring over 100 contemporary artists, this publication for the 2002 Whitney Biennial still manages to present the works in isolation.

Each spread is interleaved with a brown, uncoated text page which hides the artwork following. The image page features no text; all information about the artist is printed on the brown divider pages.

Design **Struktur Design**
Project Magalogue.4 (Alamy)
Size 250 × 250mm
 (9^{27}/$_{32}$ × 9^{27}/$_{32}$in)
Pages 52
Year 2004
Origin UK/Denmark

Produced for an online picture library as a document halfway between a magazine and a catalog (hence the title). Every alternate page is cut in half, down the center, breaking with the catalog's square format. These half pages are used for text and caption information, allowing the images to be left clear of credit details. The half pages also act as a screen to hide and then reveal images as they are turned.

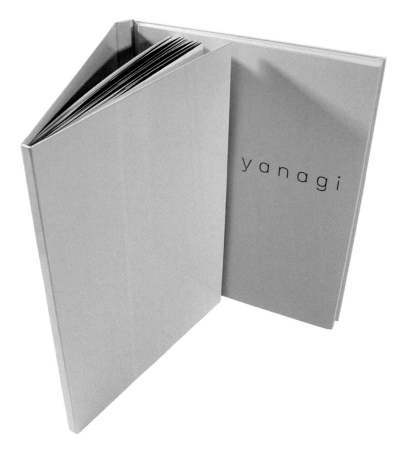

Design	**Surface/Miwa Yanagi**
Project	Miwa Yanagi
Size	302 × 230mm
	(11⁷/₈ × 9³/₆₄in)
Pages	44 + 78
Year	2004
Origin	Germany/Japan

This monograph on the Japanese artist Miwa Yanagi incorporates two very different elements. Within the six-page gatefold cover is a concertina-folded color section on the left, and on the right, a monochromatic textbook with small black-and-white reproductions of the work together with a series of essays and interviews.

The concertina section is unusual in the way the images and text are positioned, with both image and text wrapping around the folded pages, encouraging the reader to unfold and extend the spreads. The front of the concertina section shows one series of images set on a white background with the reverse side showing another series set on a black background.

Design	**Chicks on Speed**
Project	It's a Project
Size	325 × 265mm
	(1.2$\frac{51}{64}$ × 1.0$\frac{7}{16}$in)
Pages	228
Year	2004
Origin	USA

This elaborately produced, trashy book by and about the art, fashion, and music group Chicks on Speed, combines a variety of different-sized pages. The erratically cut cover is just the start of the random cut-and-paste esthetic for this book—the only truly straight edge in the whole book is the spine.

Each section has been pretrimmed to a different size or shape; once bound together these disparate sections play off each other; as the pages are turned, fragments of other sections are revealed. This disjointed style is increased further through the use of different stocks: newsprint; cheap, thin, coated stock; and uncoated.

miwa yanagi

Design	**A2-GRAPHICS/SW/HK**
Project	ISTD TypoGraphic 60
	"Primal Typography"
Size	297 × 210mm
	$(11^{11}/_{16} × 8^{53}/_{64}$in)
Pages	64
Year	2003
Origin	UK

This edition of the typographic journal gives the impression of a case-bound book. However, the journal has simply been saddle stitched, and gray pulp board bonded to the front and back covers to give the publication more stability and bulk. These boards have then been covered with a woodblock-printed dust jacket.

Woodblock type has been combined with conventional offset litho throughout the journal. The word "typographic" has been printed through the book; starting with the first two letters on the front cover, the rest of the letters are printed on the contents, editorial, endmatter, and back cover.

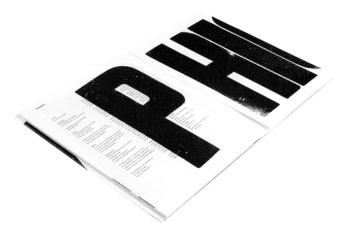

Design   **Raban Ruddigkeit**
Project   Freistil
Size   240 × 175mm
            ($9^{14}/_{32}$ × $6^{57}/_{64}$in)
Pages   476
Year   2003
Origin   Germany

The bound edge of each section of this showcase illustration book makes full use of the exposed binding. The special silver holographic cover boards, which refract the full spectrum of color, are referenced in the rainbow used on this delicate spine. The book's title and publisher's mark are also included on the spine; this is achieved by printing a fragment on each section.

Design	**David James Associates**
Project	The Order of Things
Size	185 × 260mm
	(7⁹/₃₂ × 10¹⁵/₆₄in)
Pages	176
Year	2001
Origin	UK

This unique photographic book has no beginning or end, no title page or cover. All imprint details and credits are printed on a label which appears on an outer plastic case. However, the book still has a spine, albeit a spine that will never be fully visible, especially on a bookcase. This spine keeps some essence of tradition in that is has the the book's title and the publisher's logo printed on it.

Design	**Nick Bell/Sacha Davison/**
	Tom Elsner/Hilla Neske
Project	STD TypoGraphic 52
	"Other Values Plus Ça"
Size	240 × 170mm
	(9⁷/₁₆ × 6³/₄in)
Pages	40
Year	1998
Origin	UK

Contained within the conventional format of this issue of the STD journal <u>TypoGraphic</u> are a vast array of different page sizes. Each article has its own unique graphic styling which is extended to the page size and paper stock. The one constant is the use of the same blue and brown colors throughout, which helps to establish a common thread.

    The diversity of design style was achieved by having four different designers working on the project. As the pages are turned, it is as though each designer were unaware of the design of the subsequent pages.

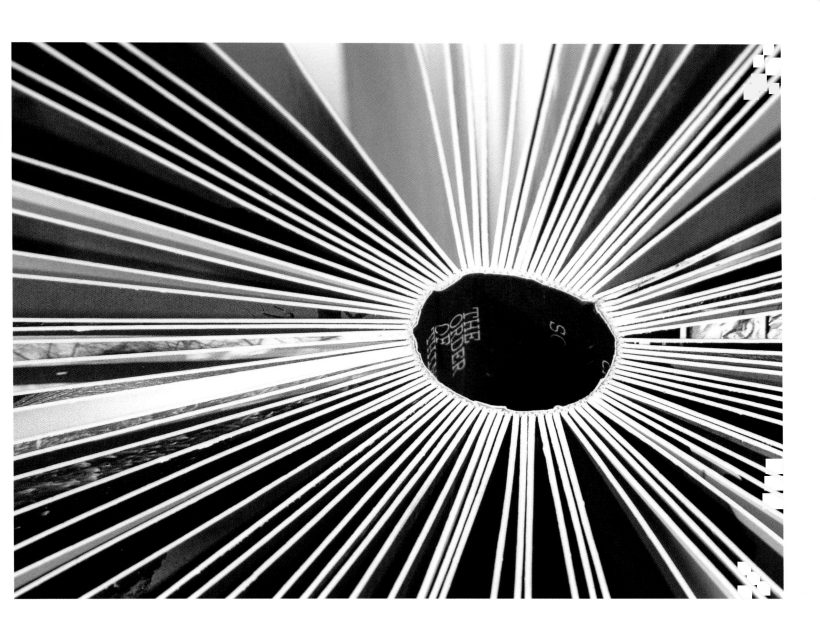

Inter
action 7

…technological revolution we … find ourselves in the …with legibility on the computer screen in mind. …text also excels in print… …which it achiev… …developed, with … Both Grotesk and … humanist elements … its special … …media applications, being its special … …to refin… design or … and high quality … with the … …A truly evolutionary typeface it began life with the four … …expect. But today we're able to offer a full … twelve weig… …able font. It may also be interesting to note that InterFa… …to Lexia. Overall, risking Interface not only … very use… …temporary. As d … played by its unusual yet striking f… …sh. We are also able … … PostScript and TrueType format… …ions. For a license … … offer, on request, support for Un… …visit www.daltonma … … this font, and many other… …0 7924 0633. …om or contact us directly, with…

…technologischen Revolu… …tet, ein beson… …rift, die…

Launched in 2001, Hawk-Eye received huge acclaim for its impact on television and the internet. The technology, which is jointly owned by The Television Corporation and Roke Manor Research, uses sophisticated image processing…

techniqu…
series of…
sports gr…
tracking…
has appli…
attracted…

Design	**Mode**
Project	Dalton Maag
	Font Book Collection_01
Size	240 × 1.70mm
	(9¹⁴/₃₂ × 6³/₄in)
Pages	200
Year	2004
Origin	UK

Traditionally type-specimen books
tend to show a font in a couple of sizes
and not a great deal more. However,
this book, which showcases just four
typefaces, presents each weight in
a variety of sizes and combinations.
      Printed in two colours
throughout, with only recto pages
printed, the book manages to create
a beautifully rich typographic rhythm.
All of the text pages are printed on a
thin bible paper, which allows a great
deal of show through. In addition to
the lightness of paper, a series of
perforated lines are cut into each
page. These lines, based on the same
grid system as that used for the
typography, allow the pages to be
folded back or torn out, turning the
book into a typographic swatch book.

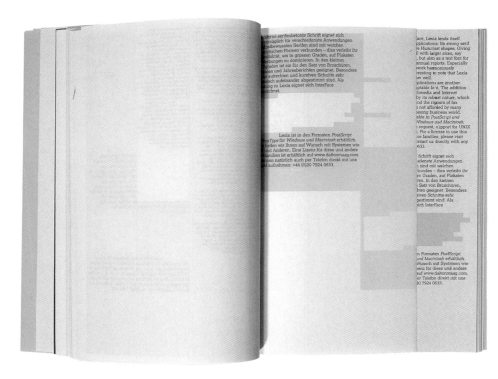

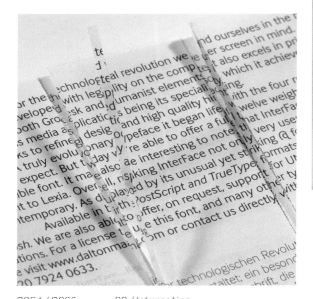

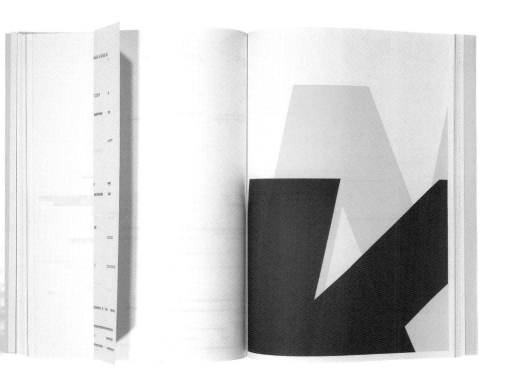

Introducing Bodas Bodywear

Bodas Believes
that what you put next to your skin is essential to how you feel about yourself. So the best start to any day is underwear which makes you feel great. At Bodas, we believe in getting dressed from the inside out.

Bodas Began
when two friends noticed something missing from their underwear drawers – the luxury brands were not practical for every day and the everyday brands often disappointed on both quality and style.

Bodas Benefits
All our designs have been created to fit your body, so you feel both comfortable and sexy. We will shortly be introducing new fabrics and styles, but we promise to never discontinue the Bodas Basics range. Our fabrics will always be beautiful quality and easy-to-care for. In fact, sometimes we think our underwear looks too good to wear every day, but this is one indulgence which is designed to make you feel great, not guilty.

Bodas Beauty
A woman who feels beautiful, looks beautiful. Our goal is to make you feel beautiful – fresh, confident, and a little bit special.

Bodas Basics
is our range of 'any day' underwear designed for busy women today. It is made of the finest quality Supima® cotton. Supima® uses extra long staple American Pima cotton to produce softer, silkier and more lustrous fabrics. We used cotton because it allows your skin to breathe naturally and we made each style versatile enough to move with you all day (and night) long.

Bodas. Simple, smart, sexy.

Buying Bodas

To check out our Basics range just turn the page. But we're not just about Basics, to see the complete Bodas Bodywear collection visit our website: www.bodasbodywear.com. Buying Bodas is simple too:
– we pay the postage
– your parcel will fit through your letterbox so you don't need to be there when it arrives
– there are four easy ways to order:

Online
www.bodasbodywear.com
Phone
0870 333 0411
Call-centre hours 8am–10pm
Fax
0870 333 0412
Post
Bodas Limited
1 Kings Court
King Street
Leyland PR5 1LE

...and Beyond

There's more to come. We are constantly expanding our product range with new fabrics and designs and are always on the look-out for good ideas. We'd love to know what you think of our Basics range and what you would like to see in the future: an essential style we have missed or a fabric you love. If your suggestions are popular then we'll expand our range. Email us at talk@bodasbodywear.com or call us on 0870 333 0411.

Helena Boas
Co-founder

Donella Taranelli
Co-founder

Design	**Rose Design**
Project	Bodas: Cotton Basics Catalogue 2001
Size	220 × 170mm ($8^{21}/_{32}$ × $6^{3}/_{4}$in)
Pages	12
Year	2001
Origin	UK

Produced for a women's underwear company, this simple catalog allows the user to see every possible combination. The model has been photographed in the same pose, both front and back, in every style of underwear in the range. As the pages have been cut in half horizontally, different combinations can be compared and selected.

Design	**Rose Design**
Project	The Television Corporation:
	Creating Value
Size	280 × 210mm
	(11 × 8⁵³/₆₄in)
Pages	32
Year	2001
Origin	UK

Produced as a corporate brochure for The Television Corporation, the internal pages have all been cut 1.2in (30mm) shorter than the cover. This allows for an indexing system to run across the inside front and back covers. An index reference gives the page number and section title, and a small colored dot is printed on the appropriate page to align with this reference.

22 Venner TV   24 Hawk-Eye   26 Visions

Launched in 2001, Hawk-Eye received huge acclaim for its impact on television and the internet. The technology, which is jointly owned by The Television Corporation and Roke Manor Research, uses sophisticated image processing

techniqu...
series of...
sports g...
tracking...
has appli...
attracte...

The Television Corporation is the UK's leading independent supplier of programmes to broadcasters worldwide. Combining two of Britain's largest production companies, Mentorn and Sunset+Vine, with one of the UK's most respected production facilities operations, The Television Corporation is a fast-growing media business. The Group produces over 3000 hours of television each year for all the UK's major television channels, distributing them to around 200 countries . . . .

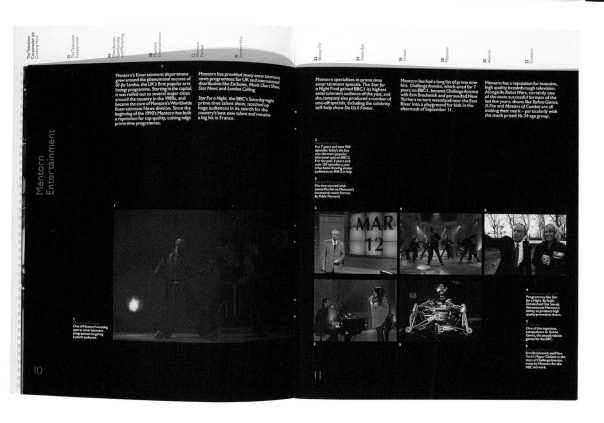

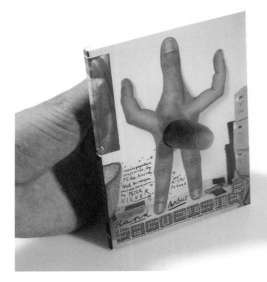

Design	**Stefan Sagmeister/**
	Anna-Maria Friedl
Project	Sagmeister: Hand Arbeit
Size	148 × 105mm
	(5 13/16 × 4 9/64 in)
Pages	84
Year	2002
Origin	USA/Austria

This simple little book features two interviews with the notorious designer Stefan Sagmeister. The internal pages follow a fairly conventional text style with one exception—a 3/8 in (10mm) hole is drilled through the entire book. This hole ties in with the cover image, which features the designer's hand reconstructed to form the basic shape of a person; two arms, two legs, and a thumb for a head. By inserting one's finger through the hole, a humorous third dimension is added.

Go to: A041   B011   B042–B043 B070

Design	**Irma Boom**
Project	Workspirit Six
Size	235 × 170mm
	(9¼ × 6¾in)
Pages	176
Year	1998
Origin	The Netherlands

Not content with producing a standard product catalog, the designer has interspersed product shots with a variety of related and, at times, seemingly unrelated images. The book is printed on cast-coated stock (one side is high-gloss while the other side is uncoated) which creates a strong contrast from spread to spread. This contrast is made even more prominent by the die-cut, circular holes that are pushed out of every page. These holes help to thread the diverse image selection together, as they allow small glimpses of the preceding and following pages on every spread.

Go to: A041   B011   B042—B043 B069

Design	**Irma Boom**
Project	Gutenberg-Galaxie II
Size	290 × 193mm
	(11.1^{13}/$_{32}$ × 7^{19}/$_{32}$in)
Pages	2 × 208
Year	2002
Origin	The Netherlands

This complex book contains a very clever hidden trick. Across the top and bottom edges of the two halves of this twin-volume book are a series of arrows that only become fully visible as the pages are fanned out. If the pages are fanned in one direction, the arrows are blue on a black background, but if they are fanned in the opposite direction, thee black arrows appear on a blue background. The inventiveness and originality of this book make it stand out as a truly groundbreaking example of what can be achieved with ink on paper.

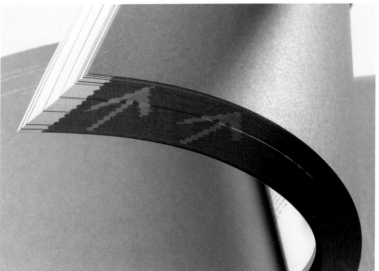

Design	**Rose Design**
Project	Westzone Publishing: New Angles on Life
Size	420 × 297mm
	(16.17/32 × 11.11/16in)
Pages	16
Year	2000
Origin	UK

This large-format edition of Westzone's catalog dispenses with the usual pack shots and uses instead, a series of specially commissioned photographs to illustrate the book list. The internal pages have been cut to a narrower measure than the cover, which allows a complex navigation system to work. Text for each of the 16 featured titles runs across the inside front and back covers, and a narrow information bar is printed on the fore-edge of each of the image pages, with an arrow aligning to the appropriate text section.

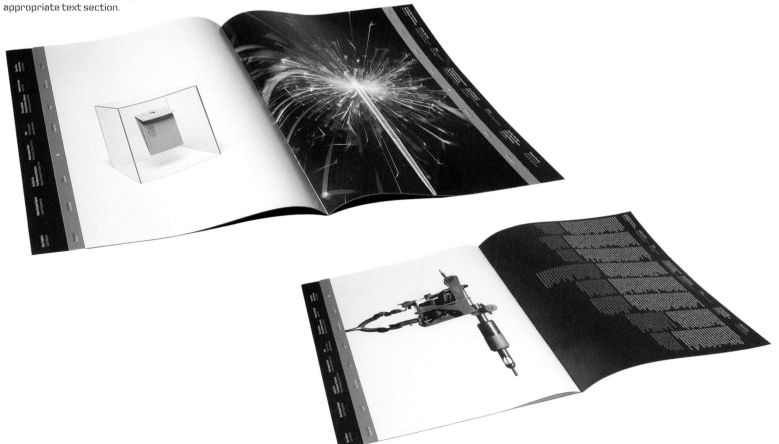

Go to: B053 B073

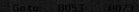

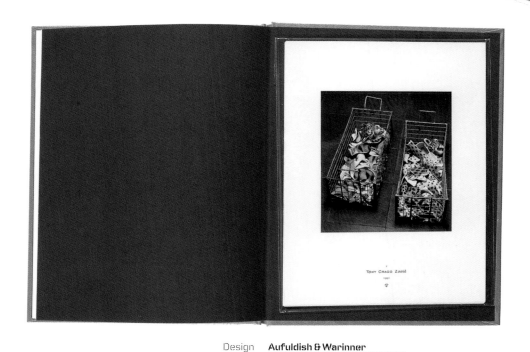

Design **Aufuldish & Warinner**

Project A Contemporary Cabinet
of Curiosities: Selections
from the Vicki and Kent
Logan Collection

Size 235 × 184mm
(9¹/₄ × 7¹/₄in)

Pages 52

Year 2001

Origin USA

Produced to accompany an exhibition
of contemporary art, this small
handbook has the look of an old
Victorian medical volume. The color
reproductions for all of the featured
work are contained within a wallet
at the back of the book, printed
as a series of adhesive stickers.
Throughout the book, the images
are repeated as gray halftones with
caption details, thereby inviting the
reader to complete the book by tipping
the color plates into the correct pages.

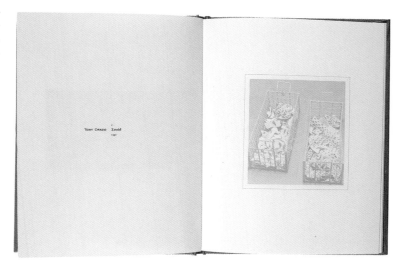

Design	**Aufuldish & Warinner**
Project	How Extraordinary that the World Exists!/Sudden Glory
Size	185 × 133mm
	(7⁹/₃₂ × 5¹·⁵/₆₄in)
Pages	120
Year	2002
Origin	USA

By combining the material from two consecutive exhibitions into one catalog, the gallery at the California College of Arts and Crafts produced a more lavish and cost-effective book. Published as a double-fronted, case-bound book, the very different typography treatments for each exhibition are kept apart. The images for both exhibitions are printed in the full-color, 24-page central section.

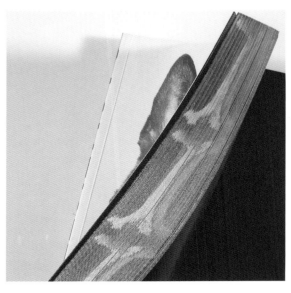

Design	**Sagmeister Inc.**
Project	Made You Look
Size	241 × 171mm
	(9^{31}/$_{64}$ × 6^{47}/$_{64}$in)
Pages	292
Year	2001
Origin	USA

This designer's monograph showcases his work in an, at times, lighthearted manner. The book comes in a translucent red plastic slipcase, and the image on the front cover is of a calm Alsation dog. However, as the book is removed, this image is transformed into that of a wild, rabid monster. One version of the dog is printed in red and the other in green; the red slipcase filters the image so that it shows only the green picture of tranquility.

The book also features fore-edge printing—if the pages of the book are fanned in one direction, the book's title is revealed; if it is fanned in the opposite direction, the image changes to three bones.

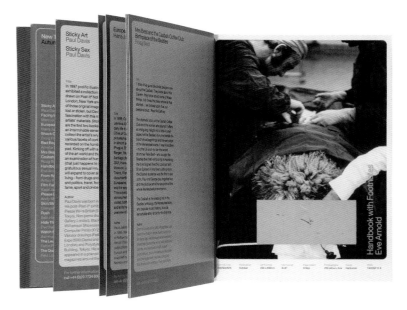

Design	**Rose Design**
Project	Westzone Publishing:
	Preview, Autumn 2001.
Size	148 × 116mm
	(5¹³/₁₆ × 4⁹/₁₆in)
Pages	52
Year	2001
Origin	UK

The small scale of this book publisher's
catalog creates an intimate
environment in which to view and read
about its forthcoming publications.
The reader is encouraged to interact
with the catalog, as key elements of
all the images have been censored with
silver "scratch card" blocks. Only by
rubbing off these panels does the
reader become enlightened as to the
nature of the book.

309/
sary

Glossary

Bellyband
A strip of paper or other material that wraps around the center of the book to prevent the pages from opening.

Bible paper
A very thin paper, usually between 40 and 60gsm in weight, often used for bibles, directories, and dictionaries.

Binding screws
Small brass thumbscrews consisting of a male and female part, used to bind loose sheets together. Usually available in brass or nickel plated (silver).

Bookbinding board
A dense fiberboard used for the covers of case-bound books.

Case-bound
The term used for a hardback book.

Cast coated
Paper that has a very high-quality, high-gloss surface on one side and a matte, uncoated surface on the other.

Clamshell box
A box made from two hinged halves which sit inside each other. Used for holding loose-leaf documents, among other things.

Coated stock
A smooth, hard-surfaced paper good for reproducing halftone images, created by coating the surface with china clay.

Concertina folded
Pages folded in a zigzag manner, like the bellows of a concertina.

Debossed
A surface pattern pressed into the page, also known as blind embossing.

Die cut
The method by which intricate shapes can be cut from the page. The process requires a custom-made die with a sharp steel edge formed to cut the required shape.

Dust jacket
A loose paper cover that protects the boards of a case-bound book.

Embossed
A raised surface pattern created by using a male and a female form.

Endpapers
The first and last pages of a hardback book, these are bonded to the inside of the covers.

Foil blocking
A printing method by which a metallic foil is applied to the page using a metal block and heat.

Fore edge
The front or open edge of a book.

French folded
Pages folded in half and bound along the open edges.

Half Canadian binding
Similar to wire binding, but the cover has a spine; the wire is bound through the back cover, which has two additional crease folds.

Halftone printing
A process used to reproduce an illustration which involves breaking it up into small dots of different densities to simulate a full tonal range.

High-density foam
A special type of foam that has a higher density than normal. It can be cut with great accuracy to form precision recesses.

Imposition
The order in which pages are arranged so that, after printing and folding, they read in the correct sequence.

Inks (specials, metallics, fluorescents)
Almost all mass-produced books are printed using lithographic inks. As a rule, full-color printing is achieved by the combination of four process colors: cyan, magenta, yellow, and black (CMYK). However, additional "special" inks, such as fluorescents or metallics, can also be used to produce distinctive results, such as shiny gold or silver effects.

Japanese binding
A method of binding in which the thread is bound from the back to the front of the book and around the outside edge of the spine. Ideal for binding loose sheets.

Lamination
The application of a clear matte or gloss protective film over the printed surface of a sheet of paper.

Lenticular
Normally constructed from two interlaced images filtered through a special sheet of plastic that has lens-shaped ridges on its surface. This allows one or other of the images to be viewed, depending on the angle at which the sheet is held.

Letterpress
A traditional method of printing type, using a series of metal stamps with individual letters cast into their surface. These are set into a forme, inked up, and pressed onto the paper's surface. The printed sheet becomes more tactile than conventional offset lithographic printing as the type is debossed into the surface.

Live-edge perspex
Fluorescent and translucent perspex that refracts light through its mass, giving an almost electric vibrancy along all the edges.

Loose-leaf
A collection of unbound pages.

Perfect binding
In this binding method, pages in the gatherings of a book are notched along their uncut edges and glued together into the spine. The result is not usually as strong as a stitched binding.

Pigment blocking
A process similar to foil blocking, but using colored film.

Polypropylene
A flexible plastic sheet available in many different colors, including clear and frosted effects.

Raster imaging
An alternative method of halftone screening using an electron beam. This creates complex, irregular patterns of very fine dots and produces higher-quality images and color work.

Recto
The front side of a sheet of paper, hence also the right-hand (odd-numbered) page of a book.

Roll-folding
A process whereby a long sheet of paper is folded into panels or pages, starting from the far right. Each subsequent panel is folded back toward the left—effectively rolled back around itself.

Saddle stitched
The standard method for binding brochures and magazines. The process involves gathering the pages to be bound and stapling them through the folded edges.

Screen printing
A printing method by which a squeegee is used to press ink onto the surface being printed through a fine silk mesh. This process achieves a much denser application of ink than lithography and can be used on an almost limitless variety of surfaces.

Sewn section
A group of eight or 16 folded pages gathered together and sewn through the folded edges. These sections can then be bound together to form a complete book.

Simulator paper
A thin, translucent paper, more commonly known as tracing paper.

Singer sewn
A document that is bound by sewing through the front to the back using an industrial version of the household sewing machine. Used mainly on loose-leaf and French-folded documents.

Slipcase
A protective box with one open edge in which a book can be stored.

Spot color
A special color not generated by the four-color process method.

Stock
The paper or other material on which a book is printed.

Thread sewn
A document bound by sewing the different gatherings of a book together with thread. This gives a durable binding.

Tipped-in
A term describing the action of gluing supplementary paper into a book.

Uncoated stock
This paper has a rougher surface than coated paper, and is both more opaque and bulkier.

UV varnish
A plastic-based varnish applied by screen printing, available in matte, satin, or gloss. Can be applied over the entire surface or treated as a spot varnish, allowing the designer to print type or images in a subtle varnish.

Verso
The reverse side of a sheet of paper, hence also the left-hand (even-numbered) pages of a book.

Wire binding
A binding method by which a spiral of thin wire is passed through a series of prepunched holes along the edge of the pages to be bound.

Woodblock type
Letters carved in pieces of wood to be relief printed, similar to letterpress. Traditionally, woodblock type was used for headlines and posters.

I would like to extend my deep thanks
to all those who have helped in creating
this book, whether by kindly submitting
work, or through their help and advice.

Roger Fawcett-Tang is Creative
Director of Struktur Design, which
has developed a reputation for clean,
understated typography, attention
to detail, and logical organization
of information and imagery. It has
won various design awards and has
been featured in numerous design
books and international magazines.
Roger is the author of Experimental
Formats and Packaging, Print and
Production Finishes for Brochures
and Catalogs, and Mapping Graphic
Navigational Systems.

A RotoVision Book

Published and distributed by RotoVision SA
Route Suisse 9
CH-1295 Mies
Switzerland

RotoVision SA
Sales and Editorial Office
Sheridan House, 114 Western Road
Hove BN3 1DD, UK

Tel: +44 (0)1273 72 72 68
Fax: +44 (0)1273 72 72 69
www.rotovision.com

10 9 8 7 6 5 4 3 2 1

ISBN: 978-2-88893-023-5

Art Director: Luke Herriott
Design: Struktur Design Limited
Photography: Roger Fawcett-Tang

Reprographics in Singapore by ProVision Pte.
Tel: +65 6334 7720
Fax: +65 6334 7721

Printing and binding in China by Midas Printing International